"Amy F. Davis Abdall [barcode: T0003892] king and actual rituals to pond .... practices (my favorite parts of the book) give embodied access to the ritual ideas explored throughout. This makes *Meaning in the Moment* truly unique. This is not just a book about rituals; it helps us navigate our ritualed world with a trustworthy guide."

—**Dru Johnson**, author of *Human Rites* and *Knowledge by Ritual*

"If life's transitions find you confused, discouraged, and stuck, this is *your* book! *Meaning in the Moment* recovers the power of Christian ceremonies and rituals in bringing clarity and renewal."

—**Mimi Haddad**, president, Christians for Biblical Equality International

"Davis Abdallah gives us the permission we never knew we needed to create rituals for the mundane and the extraordinary moments in our lives. Davis Abdallah helps us see that rituals offer us a pathway toward the intimacy we want to see in our communities, with God, and with ourselves. Practicing rituals helps us pay attention to new beginnings, liminal middles, and transitional ends that we would otherwise pass by. This book is a generous gift to all meaning-makers who want to guide their fellow journeyers toward an embodied life with the Divine."

—**Julie Tai**, director of chapel and community worship, Fuller Theological Seminary; cofounder, Kinship Commons

"*Meaning in the Moment* is a valuable resource for anyone seeking to find comfort, guidance, and meaning during transition. I've seen firsthand how these rituals brought healing to hundreds of students. Davis Abdallah offers the reader meaningful tools for creating rituals that help us process loss, move through life's challenges with grace, and celebrate the good. This book will serve as a guide for those who desire to implement rituals into their relationships and communities in order to find healing together, which is especially critical in our post-pandemic world."

—Wanda Velez, vice president for student development and dean of students, Alliance University

"Rituals do matter. In *Meaning in the Moment*, Amy F. Davis Abdallah thoughtfully reflects on the active experience and form of ritual. She invites us into her formation and journey of ritual. Reading this text is itself a ritual as Davis Abdallah pastors us through life's transitions from end to middle and beginning. Davis Abdallah helps the reader frame and form rituals that are deeply personal and highly liturgical."

—Charles O. Galbreath, senior pastor, Alliance Tabernacle, Brooklyn; associate dean, Alliance Theological Seminary

"Amy Davis Abdallah has given Christians a beautiful gift in inviting us into the transformative power of rituals in all of life. While acknowledging the vital role of rituals in corporate worship, she opens the door to how meaningful rituals can stimulate personal growth as well. She not only explains the benefits of creating rituals but also gives practical examples and models for picking up this spiritual discipline to the benefit of our souls. Her work is clearly written and impassioned from years of experience. Anyone will benefit from this book."

—Constance M. Cherry, professor emeritus of worship and pastoral ministries, Indiana Wesleyan University; professor, Robert E. Webber Institute for Worship Studies

MEANING
IN THE
MOMENT

MEANING
IN THE
MOMENT

HOW RITUALS HELP US
MOVE THROUGH JOY, PAIN, AND
EVERYTHING IN BETWEEN

AMY F. DAVIS ABDALLAH

BrazosPress
a division of Baker Publishing Group
Grand Rapids, Michigan

Published by Brazos Press
a division of Baker Publishing Group
Grand Rapids, Michigan
www.brazospress.com

Printed in the United States of America

Library of Congress Cataloging-in-Publication Data
Names: Davis Abdallah, Amy F., 1973– author.
Title: Meaning in the moment : how rituals help us move through joy, pain, and everything in between / Amy F. Davis Abdallah.
Description: Grand Rapids, Michigan : Brazos Press, a division of Baker Publishing Group, [2023] | Includes bibliographical references.
Identifiers: LCCN 2023012528 | ISBN 9781587435812 (paperback) | ISBN 9781587436147 (casebound) | ISBN 9781493443123 (ebook) | ISBN 9781493443130 (pdf)
Subjects: LCSH: Ritual—Psychological aspects. | Rites and ceremonies. | Ritualism—Psychological aspects.
Classification: LCC BV176.3 .D38 2023 | DDC 264—dc23/eng/20230530
LC record available at https://lccn.loc.gov/2023012528

This project was made possible through the support of an award from Blueprint 1543. The opinions expressed herein are those of the author and do not necessarily reflect the views of Blueprint 1543.

Baker Publishing Group publications use paper produced from sustainable forestry practices and post-consumer waste whenever possible.

23   24   25   26   27   28   29   7   6   5   4   3   2   1

For all those who need help on the journey

And for Ghiath, Jaohar, and Naraam,
who make my journey meaningful

Contents

Foreword

W. David O. Taylor

A YEAR BEFORE TURNING THIRTY, I realized that I was going to need help growing up. In the eyes of some, such as my toddler nephews, I was plenty adult, even ancient. To others, like my uncle in his mid-fifties, I was still a kid of sorts.

I felt that I was neither a child nor a card-carrying adult and, much like Peter Pan, was afraid of letting go of my youth and embracing adulthood. Being young felt safe and exciting but also stunting, while the world of grown-ups felt terrifying and impossible to properly imagine.

But I knew what I wanted to be. I wanted to be at home in my own skin. I wanted to be one thing only. I wanted to be a man, whatever that meant in God's *oikonomia*, or household. So I created a rite of passage to help me let go of childhood once and for all and to welcome manhood as a gift and a responsibility.

I emailed one of the rabbis in town to ask for his advice; he pointed me to a book, *Pirekei Avot*, that offered specifically Jewish reflections on turning thirty. I borrowed vocabulary from the bar mitzvah, the coming-of-age ritual marking that a Jewish boy is taking responsibility for his religious observance. I reworked the sacramental language of baptism with its before-and-after

1

framing of reality. And I invited family and close friends to bear witness to this rite so that I wouldn't have to do it alone.

The ritual began with a brief word of welcome, which included the following affirmation: "When a person reaches maturity, each year on his birthday, it is appropriate to express gratitude to the Holy One, Blessed be He, the Giver of Life. A birthday also makes space for a commemoration of the past and a solemnization of the future."

After this word of welcome, we entered a rhythm that recalled each season of my life:

First season: birth (0–1 year)
Second season: childhood (1–12 years)
Third season: youth (13–18 years)
Fourth season: young adulthood (19–29 years)
Fifth season: manhood (30–59 years)

Each season of life likewise included five elements:

- A Scripture reading.
- A story told by somebody who knew me well in that particular season of life.
- A reading by me.
- A prayer of gratitude by a member of the group.
- A celebration of that season with a simple food, such as olives or dates and pistachios.

We ended this rhythm with a brief reflection by myself on my sense of vocation, a charge to me by two members of my community to take up all the rights and responsibilities of proper adulthood, and a final prayer of blessing that included the anointing of oil, the sprinkling of holy water, and the embracing of the holy cross. It was all rather sensory and sacra-mental, which is not only how I wished it to be but also how I came to *sense* that something mysteriously had changed in me.

All of this being done, we completed the rite of passage with a wonderful dinner of Middle Eastern foods.

In Amy Davis Abdallah's helpful schema, what I experienced with my community was a "with-friends" ritual. Involving a kind of separation and reincorporation, the ritual allowed me to embody a passage from one state to another, from youth to adult, to imagine a new way of being in the world as a man so that I wouldn't get lost in the no-man's land of stunted adolescence, and it gave me the chance to embrace manhood without fear.

Stories were told. Things were remembered. Kinships were deepened. Physical things were touched and tasted in order to give expression to spiritual realities. The ritual, in this way, functioned like a kind of metaphor: it helped me figure out *who* and *where* I was in the world through figurative means—in my case, through a symbolic and dramatic reenactment of the seasons of life.

In reading Amy's marvelous book, I discover here a richer vocabulary for all that I did with my community back then, and I am both inspired and compelled to help others in my own community today to create rituals that might help them to find their place in the world, to know what story they're part of, and to live wholeheartedly into their true name.

I cannot more highly recommend this book to you, and I pray that God will meet you in a host of life-giving ways in the right-now, with-friends, and at-church rituals that you create with your own community.

—**W. David O. Taylor,** associate professor of theology
and culture at Fuller Theological Seminary and author of *Open
and Unafraid: The Psalms as a Guide to Life* and *A Body of Praise:
Understanding the Role of Our Physical Bodies in Worship*

Introduction

Ritual Matters

She stands in a beautiful yellow-flowered gown, prepared to do her final presentation on what it means to be a woman. It is the Crossing Over Ceremony for the *Woman* rite of passage at Nyack College,[1] the culmination of a year of readings, meetings, mentoring, and more. Looking up with a deep breath, she begins to read her story to the audience, a story that details the circumstances of her life that led to a complete lack of self-worth. Her parents' divorce affected everything, and each time someone else left her life, she figured it was because she did not deserve them and was not enough to keep them. The *Woman* rite of passage connected her to teaching and to mentors and friends with whom she could process her life and understand who she is in God's eyes. She tearfully states, "I am more than enough. God made me exactly who I am, with no mistakes." And then, grinning, she shows us her permanent commemoration of this passage: a tattoo of a cross on her ankle as a foundation for her life. It says "enough."

The audience erupts into applause. Her presentation is one of seventeen declarations of identity as a Christian woman at the ninth annual ceremony. In a central moment of the ritual, a necklace with the *Woman* symbol, made of solid silver, is fastened around her neck. Somehow, that night we are one necklace short, and I offer mine, one from our first ceremony. I think I am giving her something old, but she receives something with history that has adorned me, the leader of this transformative passage.

I started the *Woman* rite of passage at Nyack because I saw a need. Like me, too many of our graduates walked out into the "real world" still trying to figure out their identity. They were unsure whether they were a girl or a woman and often looked to romantic relationships to define personal value. With the encouragement and help of colleagues, I created a rite of passage that was soon woven into the fabric of our community.[2] First-year students learned about *Woman* from their resident assistants and dreamed of completing it their senior year. Some learned of it on a college visit and found it so attractive that they came to Nyack to experience it. Faculty and staff from multiple disciplines began to participate and to applaud the transformative nature of the rite. Administrators desired that it be marketed as a hallmark capstone for a woman's education at Nyack. Some alumnae identified *Woman* as a turning point that empowered them in their careers and personal lives.

You can facilitate transformation like this in your own community and context. My dream is that this book will help you do so.

But maybe your tradition is like mine. I grew up in a church that believed all rituals were dead. Relationship with Jesus was the only Christian way, and ritual was "religion," not relationship. Ritual consisted of prescribed acts and words done in a particular order, in exactly the same way, every time. It was boring, whereas relationship with God was exciting and transformative. My pastor, believing the Holy Spirit led only in the "now," would tell our organist the hymns for Sunday morning *on Sunday morning.* I suppose the organist might have been able to play faster if she had practiced. But the whole hymnal was a lot to practice each week.

I believed, so I joyfully sang those three dragging hymns before the sermon, listened carefully to the weekly announcements, and often walked up the aisle for the regular altar call. I definitely avoided ritual, I thought. Yet there were two main gaps in our supposed avoidance of all ritual. First, we never changed the order of the Sunday services. While the words might have been extemporaneous, the progression was not. And we certainly *sang* the same words over and over, especially "Just as I Am." Perhaps the fact that we supposedly could change the order exempted our services from ritual status. Second, wedding ceremonies were rather prescribed. They began with "dearly beloved," progressed through repeated vows, and ended with a triumphant recession. We had no desire to change that progression, and I loved the experience that the structure supported, with the white dress, the unity candle, the rings, and so on. When first asked to be a bridesmaid, I knew exactly what to do, having seen a wedding before. We thought of the wedding as a *ceremony* rather than a *ritual*, possibly because it was not boring and we believed God did something in it by the power of the Holy Spirit. Yet, even if it went unnamed, ritual was there at our Sunday morning worship and at our weddings.

The salient and most transformative moments of our lives are not spontaneous but rather are marked by recognizable symbols and rituals. We do not need to be told that what we are witnessing is a graduation, a wedding, or a funeral; we see the symbols. As a college professor, I attend graduation every year, and I love the stand-up-straight-and-get-excited quality of all aspects of the event. We know something special is happening when the bagpipers and drums begin the parade, the flags follow, and the administrators and professors arrive, wearing their puffy robes. (My blue robe with green cording and university seals set me back two and a half times more than my wedding dress did.) The graduates parade across the stage in style. The ritual marks their accomplishment and sends them out into the world.

A graduation ceremony is not necessarily Christian worship. However, I work at a Christian college, so the graduation ceremonies I participate in are punctuated with gospel songs, traditional hymns, and prayers of thanksgiving and praise. It is a worship service in our subculture.

When people have babies, they bring them to worship. Whether the babies get baptized or dedicated, parents hand their child to the minister, who offers a prayer. The end of our lives is also ritualized. I live down the street from a cemetery, and my kids run to the windows whenever they hear a siren. When they ask why everyone has their flashers on, I know the answer without looking. The mourners are on their way to bury their loved one.

If your church background is like mine, you might be stuck on the words "ritual" and "liturgy." I prefer to use those words throughout this book, but if "ceremony" feels more friendly to you, please substitute it in your mind. On the other hand, maybe your church background is completely different from mine and you call Sunday morning a liturgy. Liturgies are religious rituals. I like to say that my liturgical home is the Anglican tradition, though it is not where I came from or where I currently worship.

There is no simple, universally accepted definition of "ritual." Multiple authors have critiqued definitions from various perspectives and added other somewhat distilled versions. Some definitions are too broad, while others are too narrow. Not everything is a ritual, but we are a ritualized people. I like this definition from clinical psychologist Theresa Rando: ritual is "a specific behavior or activity which gives symbolic expression to certain feelings and thoughts of the actor(s) individually or as a group."[3] In this way, a ritual can be a onetime event, or it can be a daily action.

Tish Harrison Warren's *Liturgy of the Ordinary* is a fantastic book on how our daily lives relate to our liturgical practices within the church. She bridges the sacred and profane to make daily experiences like sitting in traffic connect to liturgical time and our unhurried God. She brings the liturgy, our worship, into our regular lives.

This book will do that too, but differently. It also intends to do the opposite. I want to bring our regular lives into the liturgy; I want to invent rituals that recognize significant events in our lives, rituals that recognize and achieve transformation, rituals that enact reconciliation. I want our human story to be acknowledged, empowered, and transformed through special Christian rituals that become part of the fabric of church subcultures.

The God Story, the Human Story, and the Incarnation

In most Christian worship the God story is central; we know ourselves as small in relation to the greatness of God.[4] Our worship tells the story of our redemption through Christ. This is powerful for us because it transforms us so that we see ourselves in God's larger story of redemption. It unites us with one another as we look in one direction toward the God of all.

But in a wedding, the human story is bigger than in other worship services. The human story is the focal point: these two humans unite with one another, and we know it is God in them—God in us—that will empower their unity through the years. We watch two people and those who love them. We focus and celebrate God in them. The God story of redemption is there, but it is in the background, just as the human story is in the background of our regular Sunday worship.

Looking at our human story requires looking at the humanity of Jesus. Because God took on flesh—God became human—all of our humanity became holy. Because God united with a human body, human bodies are now allowed to enter God's eternal presence. Because God became human, all the practices and events of Jesus's human life interest us. We want to know about his family and upbringing. We want to know whether the time he spent in Jerusalem when his parents lost him (Luke 2:41–48) included a bar mitzvah. We want to know everything about every moment of his life, and we are frustrated that the Gospels are silent about so many of his years.

Every moment of Jesus's life was holy because he is holy. But reader, he shared that holiness with us. When God united with humanity, everything about humanity was transformed. God in humanity. God in us. Like Jesus, every moment of our lives is holy. Our bodies are holy. Our life events are holy.

Jewish tradition knows a little about this. Jewish people are always supposed to think of holy things, except when on the toilet. After the toilet, they pray. They thank God for making their bodies with openings so that they can eliminate waste. While there is no official prayer for sexual intercourse, one rabbi recommends thanking God for creating bodily pleasure,[5] and another recommends blessing God for sustenance and joy.[6] They acknowledge their bodies as a work of God. Their bodies are sacramental spaces of worship. Even the earthiest acts are occasions for ritual.

God knows our lives are filled with earthy events and acts, some of which bring us toward life and some of which bring us toward death. Women's earthiness often centers on their cycle—menarche (first bleeding), childbirth, and menopause. The male life cycle lacks this type of earthy mark, so many ritualize coming of age with a "back to earth" show of strength or grit with some dirt thrown in. Men and women share other possible life cycle events that have different degrees of earthiness—education,

10

employment, marriage, becoming a parent, fertility or infertility, divorce, retirement, chronic illness, aging, death. We journey from dust to dust; we relate to the earth.

Yet except for marriage and death, we seldom recognize these earthy events as God-in-us occasions for worship through ritual in community. Clearly, some, like menarche or divorce, make us uncomfortable. It is one thing for people to pray alone after using the bathroom or to pray as a couple before sexual intercourse. But does menarche or divorce belong to worship, liturgy, and ritual? Leviticus bars menstruating women from worship. Some churches do not allow divorced persons to share communion. While we may want to allow women to worship all year and to invite everyone to the Lord's Table, regardless of marital status, are we ready to commemorate such things worshipfully?

What This Book Is Not Doing

Please do not get me wrong. I am not suggesting that every divorced person in the church must stand under a trellis at a worship service, renounce their vows, recess alone, and invite friends to the after-party. I am not suggesting that every girl who experiences menarche must be brought up front so the congregation can bless her fertility and give her two dozen red roses as a symbolic gift. I feel weird about both of those possibilities. Don't you? These are deeply personal life events, and rightly or wrongly, they are often accompanied by a sense of shame. In this book I will not promote strange commemorations. I will rather seek to honor life's ends, middles, and beginnings in ways appropriate to a Christian community's subculture. I want you to know what I am not doing.

I am not suggesting that you create something that never changes. Ritual theorist Tom Driver states that rituals can be powerful but cautions that "this power is properly used not to instill conformity to what is old and entrenched but to facilitate various kinds of transformation."[7] By their nature, powerful rituals not only transform but are transformed by their repeated use. The rituals I suggest creating are the kind that are contextualized into a particular community. They are the kind that also change as the community changes.

One of my favorite seminary professors taught me about form and function in the context of intercultural ministry. While the function may be the same, the form differs across cultures and contexts. For example, the function of a Sunday service is to worship God. The form, however, may vary from one denominational context to the next. The form is the particular way we perform the function. When we create rituals, the form is fluid, but the function remains. The form we use today may need to be adjusted in the future as our context changes.

This is not primarily a book of written rituals. Some of you may be comfortable with written rituals, while others may be uncomfortable with them. There are many books out there with rituals meant for individual use; they have something to offer us, whether we want to perform them as written or adapt them to fit our context.

Most books of rituals seem to suggest that simply using words will help people process their lives. While words are helpful, I want to go further. Research suggests that the transformation brought about by any ritual is increased with individual and communal investment.[8] Reading this book is an investment in the why, how, and what of rituals for the human story. It is the foundation that empowers all of us to create powerful rituals.

That said, I do include examples of three types of ritual. The first are "right-now rituals," brief rituals you can try right away and which require no special physical objects or preparation. The brevity of this ritual type lends itself to repetition, so performing one or more could perhaps become a daily habit. The second type are "with-friends rituals." Rituals of this type will require some preparation, physical objects, and participation. They will be a little more complex, and while they can be repeated, the repetition would be infrequent. The third type, "at-church rituals," will require the most preparation. Like a funeral or wedding, they would generally not be repeated for the same people.

The with-friends and at-church rituals may seem too formal for your Christian tradition. I write them formally because it is easier to informalize rituals than to formalize them. Feel free to adapt them by replacing items like the written introductions and prayers with extemporaneous ones. I will enumerate what I consider to be the key progression and portions of each ritual so that, however formally or informally you enact them, the essential components will remain and will empower those who participate.

I also do not expect that everyone in your context will want to ritualize all these events. I will not suggest you tell those under your care, "Participate in this rite of passage that names you 'man' now, or you will never own your Christian manhood!" Generations of Christians have matured and passed through salient events in their lives without the help of rituals. Sure, for many of us, the unrecognized weekly ritual of therapy has assisted us, but church worship has not.

When I teach a seminary worship class, we explore all kinds of worship practices, though my students are mostly Pentecostal or free-church Protestant.[9] I liken my students to carpenters with a set of tools, much like the first-century carpenter we worship. Their tradition has given them a few tools that help strengthen people's worshipful relationship with God. In my class they get a lot more tools to add to their set. They learn about corporate confession. When their church is dealing with sin in a particularly profound way, perhaps they take out that tool for this instance, and it is transformative for their people. Or maybe they are struck by the idea of sacraments and a sacramental world, and it changes the frequency and manner by which they celebrate the Lord's Supper.

I want to offer you some ritual tools for the spiritual formation of your people in your context. Participation must be a choice and an investment for the ritual to be transformational. But why not have these rituals accessible for everyone? I picture a church community that recognizes the pain and loss of miscarriage with a special ritual. When someone in the church suffers a miscarriage, they have a way to process it. Then when members' friends inside and outside the church suffer in a similar manner, they share this ritual with them and thereby help them come closer to God and one another.

I do not suggest that all these events be commemorated at the regular Sunday service or with the entire congregation. This, however, will be up to those involved. While baptisms or dedications are, by their nature and theology, properly placed in a full congregational worship service, a divorce ceremony might have an invitation list just as the wedding did. Ritually recognizing the liminality of chronic illness may also be for a smaller group, but this is up to the reader. You know your people and how to contextualize these ideas. You know what will be most empowering for participants and most transformative for your community.

My dream is that some of these rituals will be woven into the fabric of your community.

My dream is that your community will become known not only as a people who love God but also as a people who tangibly care for the ends, middles, and beginnings of human stories.

My dream is that enacting some of these rituals will become an occasion for outreach and discipleship in your broader community.

Are you ready to move forward on this?

I have set up this book in three parts, each seeking to answer a question. Part 1 asks the question, Why do we ritualize? and continues with an apologetic for ritual. We will walk through the transformative power of ritual as well as the goodness of embodiment. We will also consider how ritualizing is biblical and see that we already do it, though we may call it something else. Finally, we will spend a chapter looking at the psychological aspects of ritualizing. This material is unique because it draws from the Bible, theology, liturgical studies, ritual theory, and psychology. Our Christian perspective will draw all of this together and allow us to understand the reasons why ritualizing is powerful and often healing.

Part 2 answers the question, How do we ritualize? We are all concerned about the positive impact of what we do. This part will explore practices that do not generally create powerful rituals as well as practices that seem more successful.

Part 3 will explore the question, What do we ritualize? We will consider various ends, middles, and beginnings of life; their psychological and spiritual components; and ritual elements to consider as we ritualize them.

To "make a right beginning"[10] of a book on rituals that transform, I invite you to a simple right-now ritual. As written, it involves hands and feet; feel free to choose another body part or, alternatively, a physical object:

> Place your feet solidly on the floor, get comfortable in your seat, and close your eyes. Pray that God would consecrate these next moments. Hold your hands, palms up, in front of you. Figuratively place preconceived notions about ritual (especially negative ones) in your hands. When you are ready, turn both hands over and declare "I let them go." Now, turn your hands, palms up, in a posture of receiving. Pray, "Lord, I am ready to receive what you have for me as I read this book. May you bless this time, and may I be renewed by your Holy Spirit in the power of the trinitarian God. Amen."

Let's get started.

PART ONE

Why Do We Ritualize?

1

Ritual Transforms
and Embodies

I HAD A SABBATICAL ONCE, AND IT WAS AMAZING. It was an entire semester spent not teaching. I wrote (a lot), traveled, and had new experiences.

When it came time to teach again, I was grumpy. I love teaching, but there was something inside of me clinging desperately to the sabbatical, and I had no desire to go back to the classroom. I wanted to transition well, but transitions have always been a challenge for me.

So, I try a ritual to help my transition. I write down everything great about the sabbatical in two categories: what I get to keep and what I need to leave behind. Then I buy some candles and set them on an outdoor table. My friend and I sit there on a warm August evening by the shore. I breathe deeply and light the tall, wide sabbatical candle. I light the medium-sized white glass votives from the sabbatical flame, naming and savoring the joy of what I will keep from the sabbatical—such as learning to love aloneness and learning to write well. I place them so that they encircle the sabbatical with their warm flames. I smile again and light the small red tea lights from the sabbatical flame; they form the outer circle. Each represents what I am leaving behind—like traveling more and having a flexible schedule.

I want to savor all of it. My heart rebels against the next step, the one where I blow out the candles that represent what I am leaving behind. I know deeply that the physical act of extinguishing is a profound letting go. I breathe deeply again, overcome my resistance, and one by one I extinguish and let go. My friend prays for me, and we both head home.

The next day—believe it or not—I could not wait to teach. The previous eight months had formed me, and this simple ritual had transformed me. I thought through what I needed, prepared a ritual, spoke my joys to the flames, and physically extinguished candles. In so doing, I emotionally let go.

Rituals transform. Rituals have transformed me, and I have watched rituals transform others. The transformative power of ritual is available to all of us.

Ritual and Mystery

Tom Faw Driver's *Liberating Rites: Understanding the Transformative Power of Ritual* appeals to magic as the agent of transformation in rituals.[1]

I do not believe in magic.

I do, however, believe that ritual transformation employs something that is not rationally explicable and is both subjective and cultural. Our Christian culture embraces the mysteries of the trinitarian three persons and one essence, Christ's nature as fully God and fully human, baptism and the filling with the Holy Spirit, and the sacraments. These are not mysteries that detectives solve but are rather mysteries we embrace and contemplate with awe.

The mystery in ritual is at least partially because rituals communicate meaning, not information. Ronald L. Grimes calls it "big M meaning," like the "Meaning of life," not "little m meaning," as in a definition from the dictionary.[2] Wedding rituals verbally and symbolically create unity where there were once two separate people. Genesis, Jesus, and Paul state that the two become "one flesh" (Gen. 2:24; Matt. 19:5; Mark 10:8; Eph. 5:21), and Paul expounds on this point, stating, "This is a profound mystery—but I am talking about Christ and the church" (Eph. 5:32). Our rituals transform two into one and communicate meaning that is both present in and beyond two people. This meaning is a profound mystery, and yet we begin to grasp it even though our words can never fully express it.

Years ago we began a tradition of Ash Wednesday services at our college chapel; most students came from a Pentecostal or similar free-church background and thought Ash Wednesday was an empty ritual for Roman Catholics. The first time we did it, the campus pastor wanted to explain everything to win the students over. I strongly urged against this idea because the Ash Wednesday service explains itself through the progression, the symbols, and the ritual actions. As it turned out, the students did understand the meaning without our explanation. Some things just cannot and should not be rationally explained. At times we explain too much, acting as if we are solely rational beings. The nonrational mystery meaning is part of the beauty and transformative power of ritual.

Protestants from church backgrounds like mine prefer rationality to mystery. We celebrate ordinances, not sacraments, and are suspicious of the idea that material things have spiritual significance. We spend lots of time on sermons to spiritually feed our minds and very little time at the Lord's Table to spiritually feed our bodies. We elevate the spiritual, unseen dimensions and denigrate the physical, seen dimensions, tending more toward gnosticism than historical Christianity.

I once met a gregarious and fun Franciscan monk on the Via Dolorosa in Jerusalem. He was a Filipino who grew up in New Jersey and took confession in seven languages at the Church of the Holy Sepulcher. He took us to a private chapel at the back of the church and opened a low door. He pointed to pickaxes beside the *actual stone* of the hill on which Jesus died, saying, "Do you want some? Nah, you Protestants—you don't care about relics, so let's leave!" Needless to say, despite our Protestant rationalism, we were drawn to that rock.

We wanted it as Protestants because of Jesus and the Bible. Yet our tradition may be guilty of allowing the words of Scripture to eclipse the Word. Countless students of mine read "Word" in John 1:1 ("In the beginning was the Word") as denoting the Bible. The Bible is the revelation of God, yes, but it does not contain God; God is bigger than the Bible. The Word in John 1:1 refers to a person: Jesus. Many of Jesus's words are in Scripture, but even the authors admit it is only some of the story, some of the person, a reflection of the Word. Nevertheless, it is sufficient for faith (John 20:30–31).

I write this because sacramental mystery is based on Christ. Christ is the "quintessential sacrament" because Christ was matter, a body, and it was that matter that brought us redemption.[3] As the seventh-century theologian John of Damascus states, "I do not worship matter, I worship the God of matter, who became matter for my sake, and deigned to inhabit matter, who worked out my salvation through matter."[4] The fact that God was a body makes all our bodies potentially holy. God united with humanity through a body in order that humanity might unite with God for all eternity.

My curly headed son, four years old, is a hug wrapper. When he runs into my arms, he wraps his legs around my waist, puts his arms around my neck, plants warm kisses on my skin, and says, "I love you." He could just say the words as he smiles from a doorway, but oh, I understand it through his body and mine.

He *is* his body, as I am mine, and our bodies speak, think, and emote. Jesus's body did too.

It is mystery to be a unified whole here on this earth. We think repentance is a state of the heart or mind, but Scripture calls it a state of the body. The Hebrew *shuv*, often translated "repent," means to physically turn back or return, because when we repent, we turn back to God.[5] Jesus said "Follow me" when he called his disciples to literally put their bodies in line with his.[6] Jesus was matter throughout his life and in his resurrected body; Thomas was able to feel the holes in his hands, feet, and side (John 20:24–29). Thomas knew his Lord and God, Christ Jesus, through the matter of his body.

We also think of worship as a state of the heart or mind, but Scripture calls it a state of the body. The Greek *proskuneō*, translated "worship," literally means to prostrate oneself.[7] We do not prostrate ourselves much in Protestant worship. We raise our hands, yes, but we seldom kneel and rarely ever fall on our faces. I have seen Orthodox Christians prostrate in unison when praying the prayer of St. Ephrem the Syrian. The kids and I do this together before they go to sleep during Lent.[8] Sure, they giggle and play a bit, but I'm convinced that bodily prayer is forming us as worshipers more than word-only prayer.

I am not suggesting that you practice the sacraments or venerate icons (that was the context of John of Damascus's comment). I am simply suggesting that in the past, and most substantially through Christ, God has worked through matter, through created things, in a mysterious way. In Genesis 1, God calls all created things good and our bodies very good. Rituals can further the work of God as they embody change using physical symbols and actions. This work happens mysteriously. I cannot tell you what it was about the *Woman* rite of passage Crossing Over Ceremony that made a participant state, "Something changed in the air when we did that. I was a different person when I walked into work the next day, and

I never would have had the courage to follow this new career without *Woman*."

This book, then, is an invitation to ritual mystery, a call to embrace the transformative power of ritual and contemplate it with awe. It is an invitation to ritual meaning making. I think that is why I prefer the term "ritual." It evokes greater depth than "ceremony," and it connects us both to the distant past and to other cultures. This book includes real stories of transformation through ritual. While transformation may not always be rationally explicable, some common elements in ritual clearly facilitate it.

Ritual and the Past

When we think of ritual, we do not always think "mystery." Sometimes we think "boring old stuff." It is true that rituals have been used to conserve the "old stuff" of the past. Until the second half of the twentieth century, Roman Catholic liturgy conserved the past with the use of Latin, which is called a dead language because no one speaks it as their mother tongue today. Vatican II, the twentieth-century council that attempted to modernize the church, allowed the liturgy to be conducted in the living language of the people. That change, among others, seemed to bring Roman Catholic liturgy (ritual) into the present. The liturgy itself did not change, but the way it was enacted did.

This distinction points us back to form and function. In its most basic sense, a worship service's primary function is to exalt God. Yet the form in which this function is accomplished is diverse. Roman Catholic, Orthodox, and Protestant traditions exalt God in worship services, but even among Protestants, the diversity in form is huge. The function is static and central in the face of changing form. That is to say that changing a form, or changing a ritual, is sometimes necessary to preserve function.

While a historical ritual form may be used to conserve the past, that is not always the case. In 2021 people around the world watched the American presidential inauguration. Even though the inauguration ritual followed a repetitive historical pattern, it inaugurated a new day for everyone in the country, whether subjectively good or bad. It did not conserve the past. Rather, it initiated a new present.

Rituals are part of human history and are changed by that history; even as instruments of transformation, they are transformed when enacted.[9] Or according to Grimes, "The normal drift of human history is powerful enough to erode everything, so rituals, like other human activities, are in constant need of repair."[10] Intentional repair that strengthens and supports the function is the best kind of ritual change. A ritual's form may change even as it performs the same function. In fact, it may be different in different contexts.

Further, the power of ritual should be used not to conserve the past but to bring transformation by increasing agency.[11] Agency is our ability to act as image bearers in the world. Rituals can develop our agency by increasing our ability to value and use our voice, to be resilient in the face of grief or loss, and to be empowered to face challenging situations. Ritual is powerful.

I was once invited to celebrate Passover in a Jewish home. Passover and the Feast of Unleavened Bread are commanded in the Hebrew Bible. At this home, the first night included the biblically prescribed foods, some additions, and a retelling of the story. While I loved the apple-walnut-cinnamon mix that signified the brick-making mud, I was most interested in how the Passover story was told. *They* were not delivered from slavery in Egypt; *we* were. We do not know how early this way of retelling was adopted, but it clearly brings a historical event into the present to transform our lives and perspectives today. The people in the event are long dead, but their story is alive as we join it with ours.[12]

Ritual and the Senses

Ritual itself is not dead. Perhaps we call it dead because we have experienced rituals performed by people who sounded dead or at least bored. Maybe those enacting the ritual failed to believe in its power, and for that reason they performed it powerlessly. Maybe they believed that simply saying the right words was enough and paid little attention to personal preparation or the deep mystery meaning.

On any given Sunday, in most Episcopalian churches across the US, the same words will be spoken. But they sound different depending on who speaks them and how. Rituals are not just a bunch of words on a page. Words on a page are one dimension. The preparation beforehand, the gestures used, the visual symbols, the movements, and the rituals "wrap ideas and values in a blanket of multi-sensory stimulation."[13]

Ritual erases the lines that separate science and subjectivity, the physical world and the spiritual world. Our rituals of healing prayer talk to illness and expect it to listen, acting "as if everything is alive and personal, . . . [because] the spiritual realm includes, yet surpasses the physical."[14] Susan Marie Smith says that "ritual operates below the level of conscious awareness."[15] That is, the visual symbols and actions do something to us as we participate, though we are not always aware of the transformation. Ritual also creates strategic contrast and is situational.[16] Bread and wine are common meal elements, but when Jesus held them and spoke at the Last Supper, his situational use contrasted with their common use. Now, when we see them on an altar in a church, they have different meaning.

Visualize this: Diamond ring. Black cap with tassel. White dress with train. Solid band on the left ring finger. Blue icing bursting from a cake. Pink confetti popping out of a balloon. People dressed in all black and crying. Do you see an engagement, a graduation, a wedding, a gender reveal, and a funeral?

26

They say "A picture is worth a thousand words," denoting the complex nature of the visual. Even as I write these images, I visualize and connect with my experience of the events.

The research on this is mixed, but "seeing is believing" is not a baseless claim. *Brain Rules*, John Medina's *New York Times* bestseller, asserts that vision trumps all other senses. For this reason he urges presenters to use visual images more than text because it is more memorable.[17] Sarah Lewis writes about the incredible power of a visual image to produce a visceral response from the viewer.[18] Consider the video of the murder of George Floyd, images from concentration camps, or footage of Queen Elizabeth II lying in state. I never knew what a virus looked like until 2020, but my kids made coronavirus models with their toys. While images may stand alone, our reaction to them is multivalent.

It is important to note that when a person lacks vision, other senses become more acute. Yes, ritual is visible, and its visual nature is directly related to its transformative power. But the visual is not the only sense stimulated in ritual. For those of us who are sometimes forced to participate in church virtually (whether due to sickness or travel), we know that seeing and hearing through a livestream can't capture the full worship experience. An Orthodox Christian smells the incense, sees the icons and ministers, hears and joins in the chanting and praying, tastes the holy bread and wine, and touches the cross or icons with their lips. Orthodox worship engages every sense. And Orthodox or not, during the lockdowns we all missed presence, people, and the bread and the cup.

That is the core, isn't it? It is not just the physical senses; overall, it is the physical presence in ritual that makes it most alive. Embodiment is transformative and mysteriously makes meaning. It captures the physical senses and more. Moreover, even the power of a visual is connected to physical presence. Rituals are often visibly recognizable by what adorns the bodies that enact the ritual. A white-collared black shirt, a white dress, and dark puffy robes with flat caps are connected to visually recognizable traditions. The fact that the visual and other traces of these rituals remain in our minds indicate that the rituals affected us. The recurrence of graduations, weddings, and funerals, with their accompanying sensory elements, suggests that in our society they are lodged in our marrow, our lifeblood.[19]

In the Hebrew Bible, priests had to be careful with the blood of the animal precisely because it was the animal's life (Lev. 17:11). But I often wonder what it would have been like to live close to the tabernacle or temple. They were to enact daily sacrifices for sin in which the animal was bled out and then completely burned. I do not prefer the smell of burnt meat. But fellowship sacrifices, during which the priests were supposed to eat the meat, must have smelled delicious. Would it smell like a butcher lived next door? However it was actually enacted, it would have stirred the senses. Perhaps that was part of the point: ritual memory is physical, lodged in our senses.

Ritual Acts

Our bodies are not passive in rituals; they are active, and that increases the transforming power of rituals. In my sabbatical-ending ritual, I used physical things in a smaller, manageable system (candles on a table) to act out what was occurring in my larger, less manageable life: a transition from sabbatical to teaching. Scientists have found that as we watch someone else act, mirror neurons in our brains fire as though they are doing the same action we see.[20] This comes close to what occurred for me as I blew out candles to embody letting go of cherished sabbatical elements. Blowing out the candles mysteriously and yet completely freed me to let go of my sabbatical and to transition well into teaching. The bodily acting out, the embodiment, transformed me beyond the small candles that I extinguished.

Active learning is a key concept in education these days. We do not learn primarily by listening to a lecture. We learn best through action, perhaps by giving an active response to a lecture or delivering our own lecture. Here's a family example of the limitations of verbal instruction: We told our son not to use a razor on his face like Daddy does. I am fairly certain, however, that the lesson was cemented when he *did* use it and cut his lip. I am not saying that everyone must do what our elders warn us against in order to learn, but I am suggesting that physical action sears things into our minds more quickly and permanently than listening to speech does. That is why the action of rituals undergirds the mystery of their transformative power.

Brides walk down aisles and are sometimes accompanied by a parent or parents. Both brides and grooms put a ring on the other's finger. Graduates walk (or sometimes dance) across stages and shake the president's hand. Pallbearers carry the casket to the hearse and then to the grave; all watch and deeply experience the lowering of the casket into the ground. Parents cut the gender-reveal cake and joyfully display a piece. We act.

When Grimes studies ritual, he begins with action. He takes "actions to be the living, throbbing heart of the matter," and he assumes that "objects and places facilitate rather than constitute what they do."[21] He even prefers the term "enact" because it suggests putting into force, as in *enacting* legislation.[22] The enactment *does* something mysteriously.

In the Crossing Over Ceremony, women act in multiple ways to express their understanding of Christian womanhood. They dance, do yoga, recite spoken word, sing, play an instrument, or describe an art project they created. That action cements their learning, and then we place around their neck a necklace bearing the program's symbol. We act and in so doing *enact* womanhood.

Leviticus 16 carefully describes the actions to be taken on the Day of Atonement. Aaron bathes, puts on sacred clothing, and gets the animals. After slaughtering the bull for his own sin offering, he makes the incense really smoky, like a shield between him and the atonement cover that lies on top of the ark in the most holy place, and sprinkles some of the bull's blood there. He then casts lots for the two goats; one goes to the Lord, and the other is the scapegoat. Aaron slaughters the Lord's goat and sprinkles its blood in the same way he did with the bull. The blood of both cleanses and consecrates the tent of meeting and the altar.

Aaron then takes the scapegoat, lays his hands on its head, and confesses all the sins of the Israelites, putting them on the goat's head (Lev. 16:21). Someone takes that goat into the wilderness and lets it go, where it will die. Aaron takes off his clothes, bathes, comes out, and sacrifices rams, one for him and one for the people. The people fast and rest on this day. In this action, "before the LORD, [all Israelites] will be clean from all [their] sins" (Lev. 16:30). Aaron and the high priests who come after him are to act—and, in so doing, *enact*—cleansing for the most holy place, the holy place, themselves, and all the people.

Ritual Names

Aaron enacts atonement as high priest. His naming to the office of high priest happens through a ritual described in detail in Leviticus 8. While everyone is gathered, Moses washes Aaron and his sons and adorns them with special clothing and headwear. Moses anoints the tabernacle and everything in it and then anoints Aaron. He slaughters a bull and burns it. Aaron and his sons lay their hands on a ram, and Moses slaughters that animal too.

A second ram is the ordination ram. Aaron and his sons lay their hands on its head, and Moses slaughters it and puts some of its blood on Aaron's and his sons' right earlobes, right thumbs, and right big toes. Moses gives them bread loaves, which they wave before the Lord as an offering. Then Moses mixes oil and blood and sprinkles it all over Aaron and his sons. Finally, Aaron and his sons stay at the entrance of the tent of meeting for seven days to complete their ordination. Thus, Aaron is named high priest.

I was accepted into a PhD program, did classwork, passed exams, and wrote a dissertation. After this five-year process, I successfully defended my dissertation. A dissertation defense is an interesting ritual: I present, the readers (professors) ask questions, I seek to answer the questions, and then they send me and any audience out of the room while they deliberate. I walk back in, and they (hopefully) say, "Congratulations, Doctor!" After I make revisions to the dissertation, they invite me to a hooding ceremony where they endow me with a shiny and heavy doctoral hood to wear around my neck on top of my graduation robe. Days later is the graduation, where I walk across the stage and receive my diploma. It is a complex process with several rituals. And it gives me a new name.

While I was studying, I told my students that when I finished, no longer could anyone call me Amy. They would all call me Dr. Davis. There was something I relished about that new name printed on the name tag of my lanyard as I led a group to Syria right after graduation. Doctor. It means something—not only to me but to everyone around me. Sometimes, however, I do have to clarify that I am not the kind of doctor that fixes people's bodies.

High priest. Doctor. Fiancé. Husband. Wife. Reverend. Rituals name. The names create and reflect meaning. Traditionally, when a woman is married in the West, she goes from Miss Davis to Mrs. Jones. The practice may be patriarchal, but the name change signifies the transformation that occurs during the wedding ritual. In my opinion the name change is a special privilege, one I would like to extend to husbands; it seems that the transformation should give both spouses new names as they are ritually unified.

31

When parents choose children's names, it is often a painstaking and complex process because we believe our children's names are important. One need not read the Bible long to see that names denote character and destiny.

Ritual also names or gives voice to what is silent. That is what my sabbatical-ending ritual did for me. I was able to name what was silently occurring and act in a way that would enact my freedom to move forward.

Rites of Passage

The most transformative types of ritual are rites of passage. Arnold van Gennep coined the term at the end of the nineteenth century when he observed African tribal rituals that made boys into men.[23] Men took boys away from their home and their mother's protection in the village and brought them into the wild; van Gennep saw this as a rite of separation. In the wild the boys would be taught skills men needed to survive and care for the tribe and would prove themselves strong with other boys of the same age. Later, they would return to the village and be welcomed as men. This final rite of reincorporation usually gave them a new status with new responsibilities and a new place to live in the village. Thus, the boys had proven themselves to be men, and they and everyone in their society recognized it.

Van Gennep studied only male rites of passage, but those who came after him also studied female ones. Rites for women tended to be more individual[24] but still followed a three-part pattern. The first stage was one of enclosure at the girl's menarche: rather than going into the wild like the boys, she was enclosed with older women. The liminal transition (second stage) would involve enhancing skills she already had and learning stories about heroines. After the reincorporation (third stage), she would still occupy the same space but was usually eligible for marriage from that point on.[25]

For now, I encourage you not to evaluate the differences in the rites themselves. Let's observe them in the same way we observe biblical practices in Leviticus: "These traditions are interesting. I wonder what we can learn from them." The three stages are the primary foundation for any study in rites of passage.[26]

In its most basic sense, a rite of passage is an experience that moves a person from one phase of life to another. The three-phase pattern introduced by van Gennep is clear in two of our common cultural rites of passage: marriage and college education.

In marriage, engagement is the rite of separation from the previous, stable phase of life; the couple are no longer single but are not yet married. They enter a betwixt-and-between state, complete with multiple preparation acts for the wedding, some more amusing than others. Finally, the wedding itself completes the rite of passage by reincorporating them into a more stable phase of life, often with new names and always with a new marital status. This status is recognized by the state and has legal implications.

A traditional college education also reflects the three-part pattern. Moving away to live on a college campus is separation; proving oneself through classes, tests, and other requirements is liminal transition; and graduation reincorporates students as educated adults. Weddings and graduations bring communities together to witness the naming and celebration of the transformative rite of passage. Many Christians also see marriage as sacramental—God is acting in a special, mysterious way to unify two humans as one.

Getting a driver's license, being hired for a first or new job, moving away from one's parents, buying a home, becoming a parent, settling into an empty nest, retiring—all of these milestones tend not to be ritualized but are still rites of passage. While they may not all follow a clear three-stage pattern, they do move us from one phase to the next.

Rites of passage are meant to be traversed in community, whether they move one into adulthood or into retirement. We have incredible opportunities to mark life's transitions by ritual, but we miss most of them. Victor Turner's research on ritual revealed that a special community is formed during the liminal stage of a rite of passage. Because participants are working together toward the same goal without the direction of authority figures, a nonhierarchical community called *communitas* emerges.[27] When people say that the friends you make in college are friends for life, they refer to *communitas*. Turner also states that it is the liminal transition phase that makes the ritual transformative. And liminal phases exist not only in rites of passage. There are many betwixt-and-between "spaces" in our lives.[28]

The most commonly studied rite of passage is what theorists call the adolescent rite of passage: becoming a man or woman. Take a moment to think back to when you first understood yourself to be an adult. Was your passage to maturity marked by a ritual?

My understanding of myself as a woman was gradual. My Protestant, upstate New York background taught me that a girl became a woman when her name changed to "Mrs." and "Mom."[29] Ensuing church experiences confirmed this notion. As a single elementary school teacher in Paraguay, I was part of the *jóvenes* (youth group), and when I continued my teaching career in small-town Pennsylvania, church members thought I was still in college. I longed for marriage as a rite of passage into adulthood and still considered myself a girl. This self-understanding was encouraged by my suburban Christian subculture.

Twenty-nine and single, I taught my first undergraduate Bible class. No matter how much I identified with the sea of teenage faces in front of me, I knew then that I was not one of them. If I tried to be, I would do a disservice to them and to myself. I

34

consciously but silently gave myself the title "woman" that day, even though I was unmarried. While calling myself "woman" may seem simple, it was a profound naming act for me.

I gradually grew into the title even though I had long shown hallmarks of adulthood: holding a college degree, having a successful career, paying my own bills, and renting an apartment. In a series of experiences, some painful, over a number of years, I slowly understood myself as an adult woman. Alone, I walked the road into womanhood. Now I am committed to helping women walk this journey in community.

I wrote a dissertation on Christian rites of passage for women,[30] and this research empowered us to create *Woman*, the aforementioned rite of passage for women in their senior year of college. Before long, it was an anticipated capstone for students, a program that involved everyone from adjuncts to administrators, a selling point for incoming students.

The ritual into Christian womanhood is about developing a relationship with God, self, others, and creation. After participants commit their time and finances to the program, we begin our journey together at the initiation. There, leaders and mentors share personal stories of the time when they understood themselves as women and no longer as girls. The stories vary; some recount events like giving birth, confronting body-shaming comments, and participating in the rite of passage, while other stories describe a more gradual change. All initiates are named and blessed and enjoy a reception with their peers and the mentors with whom they will journey.

We start with naming. While the diminutive "girl" may, in our society, be used for women, participants name themselves "woman" instead. Language is powerful, and naming is transformative. In *The Book of Womanhood*, I guide the participants in this act of naming with these words: "Neither college graduation, marriage, motherhood, nor career give you the name 'woman'; only *you* can. God has made you a woman and given you the privilege and authority to agree with your Creator by naming yourself 'woman' and forming your identity as a woman."[31]

The initiation is semiformal, not because women must always dress up but because we dress up for important events. The women stand, move, and come together physically as a group. The sit-down reception is visual, with theme colors and individual teacups for each woman. We drink tea from teacups because painting china was a creative way women of the past were involved in hospitality and the economy.[32] The women take home their teacup as a visual reminder of the women who have gone before.

A month later, after completing readings and other assignments, the women bring their teacups to candlelit café tables for the first monthly meeting. We drink tea, eat chocolate and almonds, and tell our stories of relationship with God, usually in sweatpants with little or no makeup. Participants create *communitas* as they meet more informally with one another between each meeting.

Monthly meetings proceed to other relationship topics: relationships with self, others, and creation. We recognize women's embodiment in particular when we value and discuss menstrual cycles and body image. We name and release past hurt and trauma, and we experience healing. We progress together on the journey of womanhood.

The final ritual, called the Crossing Over Ceremony, is the pinnacle of the rite of passage. The women dress in formal gowns and have individual sittings with a professional photographer. Again, we do this to mark the importance of this event and to allow women to demonstrate that they are comfortable in their own bodies, comfortable with themselves. The specially invited audience hushes as each woman is announced, her biographical statement is read, and she walks down the aisle to her seat on the stage. There is hardly a dry eye as each woman offers a creative presentation on what it means to be a woman. They are all active in this passage and proclamation of their identity as Christian women. The leaders place a necklace, the symbol of womanhood, around their neck. Their bodies are now adorned. There is no question that these women are empowered to be their true selves in the world; the transformation is apparent. The transformative work that God does through this visual, sensory, active rite of passage is a mystery to observe and contemplate with awe.

Right-Now Ritual: Recognizing Our Bodies

We seldom take the time to recognize what our bodies do. This ritual appreciates the work of our hands. For those who do not have hands or are unable to use them, bless whatever other part of your body does a hand's work, or bless those who help. If your hands are impaired in some other way, do not focus on the impairment for now. For this ritual, choose to bless and be thankful for whatever the hands can do. The key progression is observation, naming, gratefulness, and blessing.

Recognizing Our Bodies

Stop what you are doing and take three slow, deep breaths. Pray, "Lord, help me appreciate my hands today." *Next, look at your hands. Start with your palms down and become familiar with the contours of your entire hand, even what jewelry you wear or do not wear. Turn your hands palms up and observe them again. Name what they have done today, as in* "Today you made the kids' lunch, comforted a friend, typed an essay, washed my face," *and so on. Ask forgiveness for anything hurtful or wrong you did with your hands today. Spend a few moments being thankful for your hands and the good that they do. Say,* "I know myself through my hands. Others know me through my hands." *Lift your hands to God and ask for God's blessing on your hands, saying,* "May the favor of the Lord our God rest on [me]; establish the work of [my] hands for [me]—yes, establish the work of [my] hands" (Ps. 90:17). *You may want to end with a prayer.*

This can be repeated for various parts of the body (feet, mouth, etc.), and the body part observed may replace the word "hands" in the final verse.

With-Friends Ritual: Previously Unrecognized Rites of Passage

It is no secret that Western culture ignores many rites of passage. More than twenty years ago, *The Encyclopedia of World Problems and Human Potential* pointed out the problems that result from this lack: "The absence of rites of passage leads to a serious breakdown in the process of maturing as a person. Young people are unable to participate in society in a creative manner because societal structures no longer consider it their responsibility to intentionally establish the necessary marks of passing from one age-related social role to another, such as: child to youth, youth to adult, adult to elder."[33] People may be unsure and uncertain without a recognized rite of passage. They may question whether their change of status is real or even deserved. By contrast, when they do occur, rites of passage usually result in greater agency and responsibility. Participants are freed to act constructively and creatively in their society or subculture; before the rite of passage they are limited, but after the rite of passage they have access and responsibility.

This ritual is a time of storytelling that looks back on a rite of passage and its transformation in order to strengthen the individual. The key progression is storytelling, recognition, and blessing of the story.

Previously Unrecognized Rites of Passage

Preparation

Individuals who desire to recognize an unmarked past rite of passage will choose a symbol or symbolic action to represent it. This symbol or action can be of any sort but must be meaningful to the individual. This must be chosen well before the ritual, and the individual must have thoughtfully prepared their story.

The Ritual

Leader: We come together today to acknowledge rites of passage that were previously unmarked. We hope that marking this previous transformation will result in each of us having greater freedom and ability to be the person God made us to be. *Leader gives extemporaneous opening prayer.*

Leader invites individuals to tell their stories and describe the physical symbol or symbolic action that marks the rite of passage.

Leader and People: We recognize and agree that you are different because (*insert transformation*). We bless your (*insert transformation*). *Leader gives a prayer of blessing.*

At-Church Ritual: Consecrating Our Bodies

In early Christianity newly baptized bodies were anointed with oil to signify the filling with the Holy Spirit. For second- and third-century writers, this anointing was for the entire body,[34] but current traditions anoint only certain body parts. Coptic Orthodox Christians anoint thirty-six parts. Greeks and Antiochians anoint only six: forehead, breast, back, ears, hands, and feet. Roman Catholics and Protestants anoint only the forehead. This practice will be adapted here to recognize embodiment. The key progression is declaration of intention, anointing, and prayer of thanksgiving and blessing.

39

Consecrating Our Bodies

Preparation

The participants must not do this under constraint; each must spend time ensuring that this bodily consecration is truly what they want to do. Preparation must include prayer and meditation. Participants shall become familiar with their parts in the service below. Participants may also prepare the anointing oil and find, purchase, or make a symbol of embodiment that is meaningful to them. This could be as simple as a framed full-body photo of the individual. It could also be more of a symbol that is recognizable to the group. If embodiment is a theme for the group or church, it is best to choose something that will be appropriate for all and has a classic feel so that it may be used for years.

If foot washing will be practiced, the leader should prepare basins, pitchers, and towels.

The Ritual

Leader: Do you come freely and without constraint to consecrate yourself, your body, for service to the Lord?

Participant: I do.

Leader: Do you agree that God created bodies good?

Participant: I do.

Leader: Do you believe that God became matter and worked through matter for our salvation?

Participant: I do.

At this point, foot washing may be practiced. This paraphrase of John 13:1–11 may be used: At the Last Supper, Peter did not want Jesus to wash his feet. Jesus said, "Unless I wash you, you have no part with me." Peter replied, "Then wash my entire body." Jesus answered, "If you have bathed, you only need to wash your feet; your whole body is clean. Your whole body is clean."

Leader: Please come to have your body anointed to do the work of the Lord. *Leader anoints the following body parts by forming a cross on them with oil and stating the following over each (using phrases from James 1:19):*

40

Forehead: From ancient times God's people bound God's word to their forehead. May God's Word dwell in you richly and guide all you do.

Ears: May your ears be quick to listen to the voice of God and the voice of those in need.

Mouth: May your mouth be slow to speak, may your words bring life to others, may your kisses bring joy, and may you eat and drink that which brings health to your body.

Heart: May your heart be slow to become angry. May it never be hardened like Pharaoh's, and may it always be open toward God and toward others.

Back: May your back be strong to hold you upright and center you in following Christ.

Hands: As with Jesus, may what your hands touch be healed and loved. May what you do with these hands be beautiful and bring about the kingdom of God.

Feet: May your feet be "fitted with the readiness that comes from the gospel of peace" (Eph. 6:15), and may God guide your feet to their right places.

Participant: I wholeheartedly receive these blessings for my body, and I in turn bless my body as I walk in service to the Lord.

After all who so desire have been blessed, leader prays a prayer of consecration and blessing for all.

2

You Already Ritualize
(You Just Don't Call It That)

MY HUSBAND AND I GOT MARRIED in New York City Hall on my thirty-ninth birthday. I wore something old: the pendant my mom wore in her wedding; something new: my ivory dress; something borrowed: a friend's gold chain; and something blue: my new wedges. We stopped in Midtown to pick up friends who had just arrived from LA, and my husband-to-be drove like a New York taxi driver as he whisked us to Worth Street in Lower Manhattan.

We met my parents and siblings in the long, narrow lobby, where so many others in white dresses waited with their affianced. Soon they called our name and ushered us into a room with a blue flowery wall where a city clerk waited. It took only a few minutes for us to declare our vows, kiss, and receive our marriage certificate. After some photos we proceeded through the rain to The Brick NYC for our small lunch reception. That evening we headed out for a cruise around the island of Manhattan.

Some marry in a city hall to elope or avoid an expensive wedding. That was not our reason. We married at New York City Hall because my husband had come on a fiancé visa and the city hall was the only place that gave the marriage certificate on the same day. We wanted to file the immigration paperwork immediately, so we married there.

Little did I know that marriage was always under the domain of the state—the domain of city halls—not the domain of the church. While marriage may be originally ordained by God, it has always been regulated by the government. I officiate weddings because the state lets me, and after I officiate, I send paperwork to the state to approve the union and issue the certificate of marriage.

The Bible has regulations about whom to marry and what to do if sexual intercourse occurs between two unmarried persons, but neither Leviticus nor the rest of the Bible describes or prescribes a wedding ceremony. Early Christians were married according to the law and then came to the church to receive the Eucharist and the bishop's blessing, which "sealed" under God what the law had already done.[1] We remember that Jesus went to a wedding where he turned water into wine—his first miracle (John 2:1–11). What is described, however, is what we would refer to today as a wedding reception. The guests are feasting and have run out of wine. Elsewhere, the Bible indicates that in marriage God mysteriously joins two people as one, and I do not mean to challenge the idea that marriage is a sacrament. However, biblically, that oneness between the two people comes through sexual intercourse and not a prescribed ritual.

Scholars believe that first-century weddings included promises (between families), processions, and parties, but there is little evidence of a religious ceremony like ours today. The promise in Jewish tradition was a written contract that established the bride price and spousal duties. In the procession the bride and her entourage went to the groom's house on the day of the wedding. Seven blessings were pronounced on the couple under the huppah, and the ensuing party lasted seven days.[2] In the Roman Empire, since before the time of Christ, marriage was regulated by the state, not a faith tradition.[3]

So, if our current wedding ceremony is not in the Bible and does not even follow Jewish or Roman tradition, where do we get it? The basic answer is that the classic Christian wedding, from "dearly beloved" to "I now present to you for the first time," is an invented ritual. It was not invented all at once, either. The ritual went through various stages of evolution and revision through the centuries, and the Eastern church has traditions that differ from those of the West. The details of the evolution are less important than the fact that the wedding ceremony we love and hold dear was invented by humans. The wedding ceremony shows that the rituals we invent for important passages can become part of society. White dresses, rings, vows—all this means *wedding* to us because, like any good ritual, we kept doing it over and over until it was woven into our shared experience.

In this chapter we will go from complex rituals to simple ones and from church and social-group rituals to personal ones. This journey will show that we all invent rituals. As we operate in our faith traditions, our cultural scripts, and our personal lives, we are all ritualizers, and we are the better for it.

Church Ritual Is Not from the Bible

In the introduction to this book, we considered that even though Puritan anti-ritualism may pepper our speech, ritual actions are clearly in our church services. Even free-church patterns are deeply ingrained, are relatively predictable, and tend to remain static. Because we worship in a holy place, we sometimes think these patterns must be biblically commanded. They are not, however, unless you practice the festivals from the Hebrew Bible.

Whereas Leviticus prescribes specific acts for priests on the Day of Atonement, the other festivals tend to have less detail. For Passover and the seven-day Feast of Unleavened Bread, for example, followers are supposed to cleanse their houses from leaven and eat prescribed food. They are to tell their children what God did for them in bringing them out of slavery in Egypt, bookend the festival with sacred assemblies, and present offerings to God (Exod. 12:1–30; 13:3–10; Lev. 23:4–8). The Passover Seder I once attended went far beyond what is described in the Bible. The Hebrew Bible tends to give broad parameters that say, "Celebrate this festival at this time with these few things." But aside from the priestly acts, the people are left to create the ritual.

The New Testament has even less instruction for church celebrations. There is no specific instruction on when or how long to worship corporately or even on what elements to include. It is true that the Bible gives us some hints about prayer, prophecy and other spiritual gifts, the sharing of meals, teaching, and baptism in first-century gatherings. All these practices have been observed in diverse ways throughout the centuries because specifics are not given in the Bible.

Take baptism, for instance. In Acts it seems that people believed and were immediately baptized. The Ethiopian eunuch is in his chariot reading Isaiah, and Philip starts with the Isaiah passage and tells him about Jesus. The Ethiopian believes, sees a body of water, stops the chariot, and is baptized (Acts 8:26–40). Acts contains other stories that have a similar progression.

Very soon, however, baptism developed into a more elaborate ritual. The Ethiopian already knew Scripture, as he was a God-fearer who worshiped in Jerusalem (Acts 8:27).[4] Later, however, many were coming into Christianity from other religions and had no scriptural background. Furthermore, Roman spies tried to infiltrate Christian groups so they could persecute them. For these reasons and more, baptism became elaborate and involved, functioning as an initiatory gatekeeper that proved commitment and protected the faithful. Christian initiation comprised one to three years of preparation and teaching that rejected one's past practices, sometimes with exorcisms. The baptism itself became highly symbolic, with aspects such as a renunciation of the devil; a physical turning to Christ (literally turning one's body to represent a turning to Christ) and recitation of a creed; a shedding of old clothing and accoutrements in order to enter the water and be reborn like a baby; putting on new, white clothing to show purity; and a first communion to show full membership in the body of Christ.

The baptism ritual became a sort of play that achieved, enacted, and embodied the meaning of becoming a Christian.[5] The priests and baptizands had their scripts and symbolic actions. To be clear, I do not mean it was a play in the sense of not being reality. The ritual acts as a snapshot of the bigger-picture reality of conversion. As a photo, it is shared with others; as a ritual, it includes community participation; as a sacrament, it points to a larger reality beyond itself. This reality is held by those being baptized, yes, but it is also held by the God who baptizes through the hands of the minister.[6]

When I was baptized at thirteen, I stood under a wooden cross in the baptismal pool, which was visible through a large opening in the wall behind the pulpit. I spoke my testimony into the microphone and then held my nose as I was dunked backward in the name of the Father, Son, and Holy Spirit. There were no renunciations, no reciting of a creed, and certainly no nakedness in the water. I have no idea when I first received communion.

Both rituals, the early-Christian one and my free-church one, are allowed within the general biblical mandate to baptize (Matt. 28:19–20). Both rituals are ingrained in our denominations or individual churches. While many Christian traditions have quite strong theologies about how and when baptism is to be performed (immersion versus sprinkling or pouring, infant versus believer), arguments for both are derived from Scripture. The Bible does not command us to practice baptism in a particular manner. Jesus simply tells the disciples to baptize. Throughout history, Christians have invented baptismal rituals as they have obeyed the Lord's command.

Hebrews tells its readers not to give up the habit of meeting together, but what exactly those meetings are to consist of is unclear (Heb. 10:24–25). Directly after Pentecost, believers gathered daily in the temple courts, ate together in their homes, prayed, broke bread, learned, and shared all their possessions (Acts 2:42–47). Yet not all these practices are regularly acted out in our churches today, perhaps because they are not commanded. The New Testament gives us freedom to ritualize our worship; there is no biblically prescribed right way to gather as Christians. And ritualize is exactly what we have done. Some rituals are more formal than others, but all are rituals, and all flow from biblical principles. Within our denominations and churches, we all have our own personal preferences as to these rituals and their proper execution, even if we do not consciously embrace ritual.

Perhaps freedom to ritualize is alarming. Why would fallible humans be given this responsibility? If rituals truly have the power to transform us, how do we invent rituals that have integrity? How do we ensure that they do not form us in a negative way? In the next section, we will explore characteristics to avoid and characteristics to pursue in our ritualizing. What is worth noting here is that our church rituals' meaning is about not only what we do but also how and with whom we do it. Let us consider baptism again.

Among the many issues of the medieval Western church, its practice of individualized Eucharists and baptisms is glaring. Have you ever noticed all the little chapels along the sides of

Roman Catholic cathedrals? Today they are often dedicated to particular saints, but the original reason for their existence in the medieval period was to provide altars where priests could offer private Eucharists (sometimes without any communicants) every day.[7] This change from the congregational to the private Eucharist made the sacrament no longer for the body of Christ, the people, in unity and mutuality (1 Cor. 11:17–34). Baptisms were also privatized in the medieval church and were often done in homes. This changed baptism from an initiation into the body of believers, who participated and welcomed the baptized, into a celebration with family and close friends. How and with whom rituals are enacted affect their meaning.

Types of Ritual

Social-Group Ritual

Whether performed for infants or believers, baptism signals belonging in Christianity. Were I to become Roman Catholic or Eastern Orthodox, they would not baptize me, because they recognize my trinitarian baptism and see no need to repeat it. They would simply anoint me with oil, since my baptism did not include this ritual act. We belong by virtue of our belief and baptism, and we act on our membership by participating together in the shared eucharistic meal and other activities of the church.

I will never forget my grandfather's military funeral. He did not really have a faith tradition, and his funeral was for family only, held in a building with three walls of windows that overlooked the military cemetery. The room had one small bench in front of the American-flag-draped casket; Grandma sat there with my aunt. It was stark, formal, and full of respect. We stood and listened to the minister's biblical readings about future hope, and then the white-gloved officers approached the casket. They slowly, carefully, as in a dance, folded the flag and

49

presented it to Grandma. There was not a dry eye in the place during the twenty-one-gun salute and "Taps."

The military is a highly ritualized social group. In fact, Laura de Jong thinks Christian ministers can learn from the military's powerful ritualization and declaration of belonging for their dead; it is frequently more moving for mourners than the Christian ritual.[8] Dru Johnson observes, "Basic military training may be one of the most ritualized experiences in the world."[9] Basic-training rituals transformed him and his fellow recruits into "different sorts of human beings" who now knew they could surmount seemingly insurmountable challenges. Military rituals transformed the way he saw himself, his community, and the world.[10]

Rituals create emotional and social bonds even for observers. I feel deeply patriotic when I attend outdoor concerts at West Point Military Academy on the Fourth of July. We sit on blankets in a natural amphitheater that overlooks a majestic bend of the Hudson River. Without fail, in the middle of the concert the musicians honor all those in the armed forces by playing each branch's theme song and inviting them to stand. I am suddenly proud to be an American, and I relish my patriotism as I watch the amazing fireworks display that begins during the *1812 Overture*.

I attended a small Christian undergraduate institution that had local sororities and fraternities. As a freshman I participated in "rush," which consisted of attending various get-to-know-you parties with each sorority. I met people and made friends; then I dropped out of the process before pledging. Pledging was mysterious and included special ritual actions. It might include reciting a pledge, lighting candles, holding hands and singing, and learning the sorority's secrets and a special handshake.[11]

While I can smile at sorority pledging, stories of gang initiation make my chest tighten and my head droop with sorrow. I did not need to belong to a sorority, because I found belonging elsewhere—with my family, church, and friends. Humans need to belong, even when belonging includes crime and personal threat. Kody Scott was initiated into the Crips at age eleven, the day of his elementary-school graduation. With other initiates, he stole a car, smoked pot, drank alcohol, and shot eight rounds into a group of Bloods.[12] This ritual is not just for the initiates, for "the Initiation ritual increases the solidarity of the group by engaging them in a collective ritual and by reminding members of their earlier status as an initiate, which creates a collective bond with the new member and each other. Further, the ritual process serves to reinforce the structure and cohesion of the gang society."[13]

Other social-group rituals are more innocuous than gang initiation but still create social bonds, shared values, and particular ways of thinking and feeling that need to be examined. I played soccer in college, and at the beginning of each game, the starting lineup stood tall on the field and faced the flag while the singer began, "O say, can you see?" Every sporting event reminds me of this practice. The point of it and the Pledge of Allegiance "is not to test the loyalty of the young, but rather, by ritualized expressions of respect, instill an emotional attachment to their country."[14] These rituals have done just that, at least for me, though they were invented quite recently.

Family Ritual

I loved Christmas as a child. Every Christmas Eve we go to church and then to a friend's house for their party. When we arrive back home we hang our stockings above the fireplace and head to sleep. Christmas morning, we wait until eight o'clock to open the stockings and then eat homemade cinnamon buns and "camping eggs" (scrambled eggs with cheese and meat that we often ate while camping). Only after everyone is showered and dressed and the kitchen is clean can we assemble again around the Christmas tree and its overflowing gifts. Dad reads the Christmas story from Luke 2, and Mom prays. Then we take turns distributing and opening gifts. By the time all are opened, the turkey is ready, and we feast on the basics—turkey, stuffing, mashed potatoes, and creamed onions. Then we either take a nap or go for a walk, preparing ourselves for our "dinner" of only desserts in the evening.

Your Christmases likely look different from my childhood ones. But like mine, they likely follow a predictable progression. This ritualized celebration tends to remain the same year after year, and its familiarity embraces us as we celebrate the birth of Christ.

Our Christmas tradition can also be called an invented ritual. At some point my parents may have decided we would celebrate Christmas with stockings, special food, and presents. When any of the elements I mentioned were missing, the holiday felt somehow incomplete. One Christmas my sister made a breakfast casserole. Needless to say, cinnamon rolls and camping eggs returned the next year. We love all the parts of our ritual.

I wrote that my parents may have decided this, but this ritualized celebration may also have "just happened." Perhaps circumstances dictated the progression and it simply stuck. Invented ritual does not require intentionality, though intentionality boosts its transformational power. Deeply formative invented ritual is usually not a onetime event but is rather periodically repeated and becomes part of the fabric of a family or society.

Something as simple as the ritual of family dinner can both create better parent-child communication and promote healthy adolescent development.[15] Once a week my family makes homemade pizza and watches a movie together, a beloved ritual that the kids consider a family tradition.

Psychologist Evan Imber-Black states that there are five themes in family rituals: "membership, healing, identity, belief expression and negotiation, and celebration."[16] More than one theme may be present in any particular ritual. Membership themes are the rituals of belonging mentioned above and include the simplest to the most complex rituals—family dinners, birthday parties, and weddings. When death, ruptures in families, or personal disintegration occur, rituals bring healing; a funeral, for example, brings people together around a shared meal. Life-cycle rituals relating to birth, birthdays, marriages, anniversaries, and other coming-of-age moments define and redefine individual and collective identity. Similarly, shared family religious rituals negotiate and express belief as well as identity. And finally, celebration rituals may be onetime or repeated events.[17]

Once my kids started preschool, I learned about others' birthday traditions. I attended lots of birthday parties with bouncy houses that smelled a bit like dirty gym socks. Kids' birthday rituals not only celebrated the child's family and age but also pointed to their membership in the social group of their class at school. Our family birthday traditions are simpler. They sometimes include a backyard get-together but always include godparents, a cake, and presents. The birthday person also gets to choose a special outing. Many families have birthday rituals that include unique birthday plates, decorated cakes, hats, and songs. The ritual makes the birthday person feel special and loved. The repeated nature of the ritual and its symbols create identity and meaning.

Personal Ritual

When I was very young, my "nonritualed" faith tradition instructed me to have a daily quiet time, a QT. The time was to consist of Bible reading and prayer following the ACTS formula: adoration, confession, thanksgiving, and supplication. My QT was also to occur first thing in the morning in order that I give my best to God. Because I loved Jesus and wanted to please God, I followed this advice . . . on a lot of days.

I think this personal ritual is a good thing. However, daily QT in the morning is not commanded in the Bible. It is true that Jesus prays often in the mornings, that Levitical sacrifices were performed daily in the morning and evening, and that the psalmist praises not once but "seven times a day" (Ps. 119:164). As a kid, I thought the ACTS prayer ritual came from the book of Acts; I realized only later that we invented both the ACTS formula and the QT rituals. Several years ago I used the ACTS formula to create an entire worship service that slowly walked us through these stages. In ways such as this, our personal rituals can shape our corporate worship and spiritual formation.

When I was a single professor, most days I would awaken early and sit on my couch to read Scripture and pray. I remember experiencing the love and companionship of God in that physical place—my couch. It was as if God sat next to me, and when I needed it, God hugged me. When I got married, that couch sat in the living room of our apartment. Now, quite a bit worse for wear, the couch sits on our screened-in porch rather than in the center of our lives. I often sit there in the summer. During the winter in New York, when life feels a bit overwhelming and confusing, I put on my scarf, parka, and gloves and sit on that couch again. I sit there because the God who met me so frequently on that couch, the God who opened and closed doors then, is the same God who is with me today. God makes places holy, often through repeated ritual in a physical location.

For years sleep has not come easily to me. I have had trouble falling asleep, staying asleep, and getting into a deep sleep. I cannot remember a night when I have simply fallen asleep and then awakened refreshed. By necessity, I have rituals for going to bed that have included aromatherapy and yoga, and I have rituals for when I wake up at 3:00 a.m. and cannot get back to sleep. While we may not always consciously ritualize, Tish Harrison Warren observes, "We need a ritual and routine to learn to fall asleep. Infants learn by habit, over time, how to cease fighting sleepiness. A regular bedtime, dim lights, bath time, book time, rocking, allow their brains to carve out a pattern, a biochemical path to rest. Without a ritual and routine, they become hyperactive and often exhibit behavioral problems. Adults aren't much different. I'm certainly not."[18]

Warren writes about sleep rituals in her chapter on sabbath, rest, and the work of God. She contends, "If rest is learned through habit and repetition, so is restlessness. These habits [rituals] of rest or restlessness form us over time."[19] These rituals show our loves. Not only do I need a ritual for sleep, but I can also make one for resting and trusting God.[20]

Several years ago I met author Phyllis Tickle at a conference. I commented on her last name; she said she was descended from jesters, and we walked together to her presentation on fixed-hour prayer, a Christian prayer tradition of scripted prayer at certain hours of the day. We waited to pray Morning Prayer on the hour, and this began a habit of prayer for me that lasted for years. Tickle had compiled Anglican daily prayers into one place to make it user-friendly. I love the Morning Prayer as recorded in Tickle's three-volume *The Divine Hours*.[21] I practiced it, and so did my mother and some of my friends. It brought me joy that though we prayed alone, we prayed in unison with one another and anyone else in our time zone, before those in Central time, and after those who were on the Atlantic. This intentional personal ritual of daily prayer connected me not only to God but to others in the body of Christ. And I love that a Vineyard church in Ann Arbor, Michigan, makes these prayers accessible to all online.[22]

We Are Human Ritualizers

Many of us are unaware of how ritualized we actually are, because many of our rituals are unintentional or unrecognized. In one episode of her podcast *The Happiness Lab*, Harvard professor Laurie Santos interviews fellow professor Peter Bol, whose students are convinced they are not ritualized. He proves that they are and that ritual calls forth response. At one end of the classroom, he whispers instructions to student A, who walks over to the other side of the classroom, approaches student B, and puts her hand out toward him. Student B responds with a handshake.[23] This is a two-second ritual that we automatically respond to. We enact many unconscious, unrecognized rituals that someone made up at some point in history.

It seems to me that the world outside of free-church Protestantism relishes the power of rituals. Muslims do their prayer five times a day, Buddhists practice contemplative meditation, and Jewish people have grand bar and bat mitzvahs for their teenagers. Closer to home, some Anglicans and monastics pray seven times a day; those connected with ancient Christianity may practice meditative *lectio divina* or centering prayer; Orthodox Christian weddings are inspiring affairs with rings, crowns, and a common cup; and books like *Prayer in the Night* (on Anglican Compline prayer) or *A Deeply Formed Life* (on values like contemplation) win *Christianity Today* Book of the Year awards.[24] Free-church Protestants are suspicious of all these ritualized activities, not recognizing the ritualization in both our personal lives and our churches.

Like me, Laurie Santos thought herself unritualized and was a bit suspicious of ritual. The premise of her podcast is that what we think will make us happy is not what makes us happy; our minds lie to us. In the podcast episode "The Power of a Made-Up Ritual," she talks to colleagues about ritual and participates in her guest's long-standing family ritual for honoring relatives who have died. She finds the ritual both weird (she drinks liquid from an old bottle) and deep (it connects her with her guest, Vlad Chituc, and with his mom, who had died). Her ritual eyes are opened throughout the podcast, and she concludes, "Most of us don't realize we have such a powerful tool at our fingertips. Our lying minds have no idea how helpful ritual can be. We dismiss them as silly or old-fashioned, so we don't use them nearly as often as we should."[25]

It is my hope that this book will help you use them more often.

Right-Now Ritual: Prayer of Compline

The rituals in this chapter are not original like the others in this book; they are ones invented in the past and still in use in the church today. The Compline prayer service is traditionally prayed just before one sleeps, but you can do this right now or wait until you are about to sleep. The entire prayer is included in each volume of Phyllis Tickle's *Divine Hours*.[26] For our purposes I will include only the call to prayer and the final portion of the prayer, my favorite parts of the Compline practice. The practice itself is simply written prayer, but I add embodied preparation that is common in the practice of such disciplines.[27]

Prayer of Compline

Before you pray, sit and put your two feet on the ground, hands resting on your knees. Take three slow, deep breaths, in through your nose and out through your mouth. Intend to dedicate the following moments to God. Voice the below prayers.

The Call to Prayer

May the Lord Almighty grant me and those I love a peaceful night and a perfect end.

The Small Verse

Into your hands, O Lord, I commend my spirit; for you have redeemed me, O Lord, O God of truth. Keep me, O Lord, as the apple of your eye; hide me under the shadow of your wings.

The Lord's Prayer

The Petition

Keep watch, dear Lord, with those who work, or watch, or weep this night, and give your angels charge over those who sleep. Tend the sick, Lord Christ; give rest to the weary, bless the dying, soothe the suffering, pity the afflicted, shield the joyous; and all for your love's sake. Amen.

The Final Thanksgiving

Lord, you now have set your servant free to go in peace as you have promised; for these eyes of mine have seen the Savior, whom you have prepared for all the world to see: a Light to enlighten the nations, and the glory of your people Israel. Glory to the Father, and to the Son, and to the Holy Spirit: as it was in the beginning, is now, and will be forever. Amen.[28]

With-Friends Ritual: A House Blessing

The Western church year begins with Advent and Christmas and then celebrates Epiphany on January 6. Epiphany commemorates Christ's light going into the world through three events: the visit of the magi; Christ's first miracle, turning water into wine; and the revelation of the Trinity at the baptism of Christ. Water is often blessed on Epiphany, and people take that water home. In some traditions the pastors visit parishioners' homes with water during the next few weeks to do house blessings. We can do house blessings at any time of the year, and it can be done with friends or with leaders. Here I have a general outline for extemporaneous blessings, but you can find more elaborate blessing prayers online. The key progression is bringing the symbol of God's presence into the room, then blessing and/or anointing the room.

A House Blessing

Preparation

Holy water or consecrated oil is often used to anoint the entrances into each room. If you do not have any, you can make your own: simply touch the water or oil and pray that God would bless it and make it holy for God's purposes. A cross and candle are also helpful, as they symbolize the presence of Christ.

The Ritual Summary

Beginning: *Light the candle, and have members of the group hold the candle, the cross, the oil, and the water. The prayers ask for God's presence and peace in the home. They invite the Holy Spirit to come and make the place transformational for inhabitants and visitors.*

Room to Room: *Begin with the entrance(s) and have all physical elements present. The entrance prayer is for God's blessing on those who come and go. After a prayer of blessing, anoint doorways with oil or water; water can also be sprinkled around the room. In each room, pray a blessing for that which is done in the room (the kitchen gets a blessing for food, the bedrooms get a blessing for sleep, etc.). Don't leave out the garage and workroom! Take the cross and candle throughout the house and anoint each space with oil or water. End in the living room. Pray for deep and abiding unity and fellowship there and anoint the area.*[29]

3

How Rituals Help and Unite Us

A FEW MONTHS INTO THE PANDEMIC, I started meeting with a
therapist. She has been a great help to me. For more than a year
I gratefully anticipated my weekly ritual of telehealth therapy.
I took notes; I enacted her suggestions; I read the books she
recommended; I learned to listen to my body, think differently,
and love myself. My time with my therapist has transformed
my relationship to the anxiety I have struggled with for years.
Weekly therapy is a ritual in itself.[1] It helps overwhelmed people
find a time and a place to pay attention to things like anxiety.
Each weekly appointment corrals anxiety so it does not stam-
pede into every moment of every day. For me, each week's appointment was somewhat different from the other ones, but
there were still specific actions and topics that created a golden
thread of ritual similarity.

I am happy (and sad) to report that I am down to meeting
with my therapist every other week. The skills and, yes, rituals that I learned have become part of my life's fabric, and I
practice them daily. I find psychology quite helpful in life and
have experienced psychology dovetailing with theology in profound ways. My therapist and our weekly ritual help me. Ritual

psychology and ritual theory show that ritual not only helps individuals but also helps and unites communities.

Ritual Helps

We all turn to ritual in times of loss, particularly the loss of life.[2] Whether unanticipated or following a long illness, we are a swirl of many strong and contradictory emotions when we face death. We are grateful for something to do—choose the casket, plan the funeral or memorial—because at least we have agency in that arena. Planning it all may bring up old and new family conflict, but at least there is something to do rather than sit and be overwhelmed with grief, anger, joyful memories, surprise, hopelessness, and more. It is helpful to have structured actions that create a space apart from regular life and its overwhelming emotions. Ritual helps us do that.

We Christians know that even though we are not in control, God gives us agency. We can do something about the losses in our lives. In the fall of 2003 I experienced a perfect storm of loss. My paternal grandfather died the same week my maternal grandfather went into the hospital. Three weeks later he came home on hospice, the same week my nephew was born and underwent emergency open-heart surgery at four days old. Mom read Psalm 139 with my paternal grandfather before he passed, we read it together while my nephew was on the heart-lung bypass machine, and I read it three weeks later at my grandfather's funeral, which was held on the same day my nephew came home from the hospital. A simple ritual of Bible reading gave us something meaningful to do when faced with deep loss.

Ritual Helps Regulate Emotions

I have an easy and strong connection to negative emotions and loss; I am practiced at sadness and grief. So, when I attended the funeral of a teenager whom I barely knew, her life snuffed away too early, I was very sad. Her parents stood before us; Dad was composed, and Mom was holding back the tears, but they did not speak of the sadness. They moved immediately to hope. I found it jarring.

Please understand me: I agree with what Paul states in 1 Thessalonians 4:13 about our hope for resurrection and life eternal as Christians. He writes, "But we do not want you to be uninformed, brothers and sisters, about those who have died, so that you may not grieve as others do who have no hope" (NRSVue). Yes, we hope, but we still grieve, and the funeral is a time to mourn together. Paul states that our grief is different, yet he surely implies that we still grieve.

Grief in the face of the untimely loss of a child is severe and overwhelming. If we let it, the ritual of a funeral offers a "guided way to both express and contain strong emotions."[3] The photos of the deceased, the casket itself, the familiar words of Scripture—all this evokes the emotions that a grieving dad may not feel safe enough to express at home with the other kids; he gets to express it here. At the funeral Mom might weep and say all she wished to say while the child lived. The expression of grief is contained in a specific time rather than in every moment. The ritual can be a sort of appointment with all the feelings of grief and is a safe place to express emotions.[4] Thus, "ritual may provide a way for people to find *support and containment for strong emotions*."[5]

Further, the symbols and actions of the ritual offer aesthetic distance from the emotions.[6] The body is made to look as if it is only asleep; the flowers cover the ugliness of death; the shiny casket that is lowered into the earth is only a shadow of the full loss of life. Both lowering the casket and walking away point symbolically to the letting go that happens much more slowly in reality. Ritual "creates an opportunity to re-live emotional experiences in an aesthetic and distanced way."[7] It creates an opportunity for the person to symbolically enact or undergo a change or experience. The symbolism is close enough to activate the emotional process but also at a safe distance so as not to overwhelm. Acting symbolically both engages and protects the mourner. Funerals that move to hope too quickly stifle this possible transformative power of the ritual.

While the loss that comes from death causes deep grief, any change, even positive change, involves some loss. Mary Elizabeth Kenel writes, "Change inevitably leads to disturbances on the physical, social and psychological planes of our existence."[8] She believes that ritual helps us process the complex emotions that accompany the loss of the old and the embrace of the new.[9] We tend to be good at ritually embracing the new but not as good at saying goodbye to the old. The church celebrates weddings, but we leave it to bridesmaids and groomsmen to create bachelor and bachelorette parties. While I was not a go-out-and-get-drunk-before-you-tie-the-knot kind of bachelorette, I would have benefited from a ritual that said goodbye to thirty-nine years of singleness. Had I ritually recognized the end of those good years and symbolically let go, the transition to marriage may well have been easier for me. It would have been a safe opportunity to express complex emotions. For this reason, the final portion of this book follows William Bridges's model in starting with ends rather than beginnings.[10] Acknowledging and grieving the loss of the old enables us to embrace the new.

Rituals not only help adults deal with strong emotions; they also aid the young. Adolescence is a time of transition that involves conflicting emotions, the loss of childhood, and the gain of maturity. When adolescents use personal rituals to regulate emotions, the rituals help to stabilize their identity.[11] This need to stabilize emotions and identity may be the reason that rites of passage were created.

Rituals can be particularly effective when they allow participants to verbalize their experiences and emotions. Ritual theorist Mary Douglas tells the story of how a ritual brings peace to a village as each side airs its grievances during the ritual healing of an individual. Another ritual helps a woman who had a difficult labor by singing the challenges and the victory of bringing a child into the world.[12] It seems that ritual offers cathartic opportunities to pay attention to strong emotions and verbalize the stories or conflict to which the strong emotions point. Paying attention and verbalizing improves the situation.

Rituals not only help us process complex emotions and offer catharsis; they also alleviate anxiety.[13] The physical communal actions often used in ritual increase the production of endorphins, also known as the pleasure hormones, and these hormones lessen anxiety. This is especially clear with athletes whose pregame rituals limit their anxious thoughts by helping them turn their focus from anxiety to the ritual.[14] Alleviation of anxiety through ritual is closely related to the way ritual creates agency.

While athletes turn their focus from anxiety to a ritual, Christians can use a ritual to turn their focus from anxiety to God. For me, a weekly ritual of Sabbath keeping has helped alleviate my anxiety. I get anxious when there is too much to do and too little time to do it. Sabbath celebrates the truth that my work will not all get done; God is the Finisher, not me. At the heart of this practice, of doing no regular work on one day in seven, lies trust in God. Leviticus 25 calls the agrarian Israelite society not only to do no regular work one day a week (see Exod. 20:8–11) but also not to plant every seventh year. As with the manna in the wilderness, God will provide food from what grows on its own. We have no evidence that they in fact did this; 2 Chronicles 32 says that the land enjoyed its Sabbath rests when the Israelites were exiled, not when they lived in the land. Not planting for a year would require that people put their whole trust in God to provide; like us, they were not that good at trusting in God.

I do not Sabbath one year in seven, but every seventh day I do no regular work, and I try to strengthen my trust-in-God muscle. I do my best to follow number four of the Ten Commandments and turn my thoughts from my work and anxiety to the trustworthiness of God. It is not perfect, but the Sabbath ritual of trust tends to make me a less anxious and more God-trusting person on the other six days.[15]

Ritual Creates Agency

I recently went to a Tricky Tray Raffle with my boys, who were most excited that we put in five golden tickets for the Nintendo Switch. My younger, curly-headed boy was crestfallen when we did not get it. We won the $100 Best Buy gift card but not the Nintendo Switch or any other item for which we put in tickets. "We didn't get anything we wanted," he moaned as he hung his head. Certainly, the grief of losing a raffle is minor compared to the losses previously mentioned. Yet Harvard Business School professors Michael Norton and Francesca Gino set out to see if a ritual might help alleviate the grief of raffle loss. What would it be like to participate in their experiment?

Imagine you are gathered with twelve other people in a room. The leader tells you that one of you is about to win $200 and be allowed to leave the room early. Then they invite you to write why $200 would be meaningful for you and how you would spend it. By the time you are done writing, you want that $200 and look around at the others competitively. The person sitting next to you is randomly selected to receive the $200 and leaves. After the loss, you are put in a private cubicle and invited to perform a ritual. First, you draw how you are feeling on a piece of paper. Then you put a pinch of salt on the paper and tear it up, and finally, you count to ten in your head five times. When the researchers evaluate your level of grief at the loss, it is significantly lower than that of those who did not perform the ritual. More than that, your ritual gave you a feeling of control and agency.[16]

Norton and Gino's study even found that ritual reduced grief and increased feelings of control whether or not the individuals believed rituals worked. It was not the specific ritual actions that helped; it was simply the performance of a ritual. Further, calling an action a ritual increased its power.[17] This finding is closely related to comments in the previous chapter about embodiment. Drawing a picture, throwing salt, and tearing up the picture are ways of embodying grief that actually alleviate it.

Rituals offer some control over the unknown,[18] and simply completing the actions of the ritual assists in generating a feeling of agency and order.[19] Writing about how rituals help us in times of transition, Kenel states, "One of the positive features of ritual is its potential to change individuals, families, or other groups while at the same time allowing the participants to feel secure and stable, able to maintain a grip on their situation."[20] Norton and Gino's findings are not unique; many others would agree that ritual creates agency or a feeling of control in challenging situations. In fact, Joanna Wojtkowiak asserts that the symbolic distance in ritual, mentioned above, protects those involved and creates a feeling of being in control of one's emotions.[21]

Finally, according to Susan Marie Smith, ritual shifts and mediates power in redemptive and healing ways.[22] While she generally refers to ritual mediating God's power redemptively, we can apply this to ritual mediating *human* power redemptively as well. To have agency and a sense of some control in times of great grief or other overwhelming circumstances is helpful to humans.

The year my grandfathers died, I attended a Messianic Jewish worship service. In the middle of the service, all those who had lost someone to death over the past year were invited to stand and they read "The Mourner's Kaddish." The kaddish is like a psalm that praises God. It seems disconnected to loss, but there was something about others acknowledging my loss that helped me pay attention to and process the grief. As I stood with others, it created a community of mourners, and somehow we knew we would make it through this. It gave us agency.

Ritual Constructs an Alternative World

I love Christian rituals that tell a story, and during Holy Week, I have told the story of the last week of Christ's life from the perspective of his mother, Mary. It is a combination of Maundy Thursday and Good Friday traditions produced for the seminary chapel. We begin with "hosanna" songs inspired by the triumphal entry, and I enter in costume, telling the story of Sunday to Thursday. After my exit, there is the reading of the Last Supper from John 13, and people are invited to wash one another's feet as Jesus washed the disciples' feet. I enter after another song and tell the story of Jesus's arrest as if Peter came to tell me the story on Friday morning. We rush to see Jesus's trial, exiting the chapel, and then have a readers' theater of John 18–19, with actors reading the parts of the narrator, Pilate, and Jesus while the congregation reads the parts of the Jews and the crowds who shout, "Crucify him!" I return and tell how I watched my son walk to the cross and be crucified. With his last words, he entrusts John to care for me, and we all leave in silence. The service provides a visceral experience of the last week of Christ's life, into which we all enter.

Rituals invite others into an alternate world, freeing them to experience something greater than themselves and to be carried along by the flow.[23] Ritual works as long as it does not call attention to itself, as long as participants effortlessly enter into the story and are taken to another place without realizing it.[24] My son reads voraciously and is often so connected to the book's alternative world that he is unconscious of this world. When I was in high school, we traveled to New York City and watched the Broadway show *Sarafina!* I do not remember the plot, but I do remember sitting in the front row of the balcony and being taken to another world. I was so involved in the show that I lost track of time and place; I was mesmerized and was wherever they were. Intermission shocked me out of that world. The alternate world that ritual creates can be like this; it operates below the level of conscious awareness.[25]

Ritual allows us to abandon rational control for a moment[26] and experience the liberation of an alternative world separated from ordinary life.[27] The escape lasts for just a moment; we will return to ordinary life. But we return transformed by the experience of the ritual. Ritual creators must show care not to smash the alternative world with a misplaced joke or word. Once, when we did Mary's perspective on Holy Week, the John 13 reader interrupted the progression by adding a modern illustration. The first-century world was cracked and no longer viscerally available to the people. Unfortunately, this curtailed the ritual's ability to help the participants experience the alternative world and be transformed.

Ritual Offers Structured Performance

I will use the word "performance" to describe Christian ritual even though I disliked it when I first heard the word applied to worship. It was after an evening seminary class, and I was driving a fellow student home, a student whom we wished the professor managed a little better; she was older, had wild hair, and interrupted a lot. She called the professor's teaching a performance, and I was offended. The fire rose in my belly as I emphatically declared his teaching had nothing to do with performance. He would be horrified if we thought it did. It was only worship.

I should probably find her and apologize. After twenty years of teaching college, I now know that whenever I teach, it is both worship and performance. While I teach theology and worship for the glory of God, I still employ tricks of the trade to keep students' attention and to increase engagement. I perform teaching. When I lead a chapel, I seek to be a lead worshiper but am also careful with gestures, movements, words, and theology. Teaching and leading worship involve performing.

Perhaps "performance" is hard for us because the word has an element of self-aggrandizement: if I perform well, others will like me. For many of us, performance smacks of the fake. In this book, structured performance is simply a series of actions in a ritual that have an intentional structure that drive toward a particular goal. Think of it as a play, as theater. A deeply meaningful drama can transform actors as well as viewers. The performance is structured: some parts of the narrative are included and others left out in order to facilitate the goal and the transformation. The planned structure of a ritual offers safe distance, and the oft-repeated actions embrace us by their structure; we are not in the chaos, and we have a sense of agency.

I dream of teaching a travel class in Jerusalem in which we would celebrate Holy Week with Orthodox Christians. Like the fourth-century writer Egeria, we would be pilgrims observing and participating in the reenactment of the last week of Christ's life. Many are unfamiliar with the drama in Orthodox Holy Week, which begins with parading around the church with palms on Palm Sunday. The priest uses an aspergillum to throw drops of holy water on the people and the palms. Sunday, Monday, and Tuesday evening contain the celebrations of bridegroom services, which are meditations on being ready for the bridegroom like the wise virgins in Matthew 25:1–13. On Wednesday is the healing service, where all are anointed with the blessed oil, but Thursday is when the real performance begins. An unlit candelabra with twelve candles is visible behind the priest as he washes others' feet. One candle is lit after each reading of the Gospel accounts, from the Last Supper to the crucifixion. In the middle of the service, the priest carries a cross around the sanctuary, singing that today, hung upon a tree is he who hung the stars in place. Then they place the icon of Christ on the cross. Friday morning, the women gather at the church with flowers to decorate the bier, something like a hollow coffin, into which the icon of the deceased Christ, or *epitaphios*, will be placed when he is taken from the cross later that day at 4:00 p.m. Good Friday is the most beautiful service. All sing sad songs of mourning around the bier with *epitaphios* and then walk around the outside of the church, following it. The pallbearers hold the bier over the people's heads as they reenter the church. They enter under the death of Christ. On Saturday morning the priest throws rose petals around the sanctuary to celebrate Christ's triumph over death, the harrowing of Hades.

On Saturday afternoon, however, the drama reaches its peak. With no match and no tinder, the priest enters the tomb of Christ in the packed Church of the Holy Sepulcher. He comes out with miraculous holy fire on beeswax candles. All those present reach for the fire with their candles, and the fire spreads through the church, down the streets in the old city, to Bethlehem and other cities in Palestine, and to the rest of the Orthodox world. They transport the candles in planes. Even if one is skeptical about the miracle of the fire, one is still caught up in the joyous performance surrounding the resurrection.

This structured performance, the physical and symbolic enactment, pays attention to the last week of Christ's pre-resurrection life in a way that points to mystery meaning and offers a safe distance from the actual event. We are invited to enter the rhythm and bodily remember and participate in the past event. Celebrating the church year by following the life of Christ from Advent through Christmas, Epiphany, Lent, and Easter does the same, in that by continuous practice we are formed by participation. This ritual, then, is "anamnesis," a special kind of remembering that allows us to participate in a past event, make the event present, and anticipate the future, all in one act. Anamnesis is deeply connected to partaking together in the Lord's Supper. We celebrate the past action of God in Christ at a table, participate in God's current action at a table, and anticipate God's future action at the wedding-supper table.

Structured performance is carefully tied to that which is familiar. According to the Synoptic Gospels, Jesus used a familiar yearly Passover meal to communicate about ensuing events and to encourage future remembrance in what the Bible calls the Lord's Supper.[28] This ritual is both situational and strategically contrasted to the familiar. In the same way, a birthday dinner is on a specific day (situational) and is familiar as a regular meal but different due to the special dessert, singing, and gifts.[29] The structured performance needs to have the right balance of familiarity and strategic contrast.

Rituals have specific bodily actions or performances that enhance their transformational character.[30] Immersion baptisms include cleansing with water as the individual walks in one side and out another in new clothes, bodily acting out newness of life. These ritual actions viscerally parallel what has invisibly occurred in a believer's life when they converted.

72

They highlight their conversion by means of the baptismal ritual, and they will always remember the day, the place, their clothes, the ministers, and the feel of the water on their body. All of their being focuses on this ritual event, and they often intuitively follow the structure.[31] Even a ritual as simple as bringing flowers or candles to Manhattan after 9/11 is structured performance that gives us a sense of agency when the world swirls.

Ritual Unites

I missed my paternal grandmother's funeral. I said goodbye to her as she lay in the nursing home, her breath short and her mind absent. She passed away that night, and three days later I was on a plane to Greece to lead students in the Footsteps of Paul. I went because my adventurous grandma would have told me to go, but I was sad not to be with my family in mourning. As my grandfather had already passed on, she was the last to unite her five children and their families; no one is planning a family reunion, since they are busy with their own kids and grandkids. Rituals such as funerals, weddings, baptisms, and graduations often act as a family reunion of sorts, bringing family members together to honor a loved one.

Rituals can powerfully unite beyond physical proximity. Individually, they unite all aspects of the self; through symbols, they unite the symbolic and actual; communally, they unite people as they work together and are formed into a community.

Ritual Unites All Aspects of the Self

In chapter 1, I suggested that humans are a unified whole, not a dualistic combination of the physical and the immaterial. To state that ritual unites all aspects of the self is not to deny that we are already united. It is rather to assert that ritual uniquely engages all aspects of the self in a manner that other actions do not. Ritual offers an opportunity to act out our unity, because it engages all aspects of our being at once.

Ritual embodiment makes the invisible visible, as when a believer is baptized. The individual's prior cleansing and transformation through faith and conversion and their walking in newness of life have been largely invisible. When a believer is cleansed and transformed through the waters of baptism, the ritual unites the inner and outer reality and links the nonverbal and verbal aspects of a person.[32] This is just the beginning.

Psychologists often use the categories of bottom-up and top-down thought processes. Essentially, this refers to thoughts and actions that are instinctual (bottom-up) and thoughts and actions that are learned (top-down). When I was sitting and drinking coffee beside Yellowstone Lake and a hungry bear came lumbering around the corner, my bottom-up process told me to run, which I did. I ran to my car, opened the door, and got in. The ranger later told me how lucky I was that the bear did not chase and maul me. I should have used top-down thought action, remembering that the bear is more interested in berries than in me but tends to chase after living beings that run away. Had I kept my head down, not met the bear's eyes, and let it lumber on by, I may well have been safer.

In my Yellowstone bear story, top-down processing would have served me better than bottom-up, but of course, this is not always the case. Sometimes we instinctively or intuitively know which course of action to follow, and bottom-up processing is better than learned intellectual processing. In ritual, both forms of processing are engaged. Bottom-up pertains to meaning and our intuitive knowing: we instinctively understand and process aspects of the ritual, particularly the physical ones. Top-down processing is also engaged as we intellectually process the more psychological and verbal aspects of the ritual.[33] Ritual unites a person's two ways of processing thoughts and actions.

Ritual also unites a person's contradictory emotions. A wedding has both great loss and great joy, and we experience both in the ritual.[34] As in the anamnesis of the Lord's Supper, ritual further unites past, present, and future in one act.[35] Ritual theorists usually analyze rituals by dichotomous categories loosely analogous to thought and action. Theorist Catherine Bell suggests, however, that ritual itself unites the dichotomy and that thought and action are mutually interdependent; neither could exist without the other.[36] This echoes and more deeply illuminates the power of embodiment to unify the self in ritual.

Yes, a human is already a unified whole. Ritual recognizes this and creates a unique opportunity to act out that unity.

Ritual Symbols Unite the Symbolic and Actual

Every year, graduates are confused: does the tassel go on the right or on the left? I have worn regalia to multiple graduations, and I still do not know the answer to this question until I put my cap on. My cap's tassel is permanently affixed to the left side, symbolizing having graduated. I can then tell students to wear it on their right until they graduate. Regalia and tassels are just one group of symbols that are commonly recognized in our society.

Anthropologist Mary Douglas asserts that symbols help coordinate brain and body, as shown when an actor acts more authentically in costume and with props than without either.[37] Further, "symbols embrace meaning that cannot always be easily expressed in words."[38] Kathy Mattea's song "I Wear Your Love" is a longtime favorite of mine. It is about how a freeing love can empower and adorn a person in life. I took it literally in my long-distance dating relationship. My now-husband and I dated for two years, separated by six time zones and before the internet was reliable where he lived. When I missed him deeply, I would wrap myself in a scarf he had given me or wear perfume he had bought me. The scarf and perfume were simply symbols of our relationship, but putting them on ritually wrapped me in his love, unifying the symbolic and actual.

Rituals are multisensory, and their sensory nature includes symbols that activate sensory memory, thereby connecting us to previous rituals and to those with whom we participated.[39] In the *Woman* Crossing Over Ceremony, each participant is adorned with a necklace bearing a solid silver symbol of womanhood. That visual symbol has appeared in all the printed and electronic material from the rite of passage. The women who give the necklaces are wearing the same symbol of womanhood, having previously received it. This unites current participants with past ones.

Paul Tillich argues that symbols participate in the power and meaning of that which they represent.[40] That is, the *Woman* necklace mysteriously participates in the power and meaning of the entire rite of passage. This participation is clear when women who have recently completed the rite of passage tell stories of wearing the necklace to encourage themselves and to remind themselves of their identity as they head into challenging situations like job interviews. Tillich states the main function of symbols is to open up "levels of reality which otherwise are hidden and cannot be grasped any other way."[41] In this sense symbols create meaning.

Symbols must be carefully chosen in order for them to do their unifying work. They must be closely related to that which they represent without being too close, and far enough away without being too far.[42] For this reason they also help provide a safe distance for participants. Further, symbols can *become* meaningful by the way they are used in the rite.[43]

Symbols have unique power to unify the object with what it represents.

Ritual Unites People

In chapter 2, I mentioned Kody Scott's initiation into the Crips when he was eleven. I have two sons, and what happened to Scott at such a tender age makes me feel tight and a bit nauseous. Thus far I have primarily written about the power of ritual for positive change, but this example shows that ritual may also facilitate a negative change. It does, however, give Scott something he lacked: belonging to a community.

Scott's initiation ritual both created and reaffirmed that which was sacred for the gang.[44] It taught power over the Bloods, solidarity, and loyalty in not "snitching" on each other. Scott was not the only one who absorbed these values through the ritual; all members participated. Initiating another gang member reminded others of their own initiation and unified them all through collective participation.[45] Rituals unite people with one another.

The union in Scott's initiation did not come simply from the participants being in the same place; the union also came from bonding together. If we turn away from the gang initiation and consider other types of rituals, we can note that rituals unite people emotionally and in even deeper ways.[46] Anthropologist Roy Rappaport writes, "In many rituals strong emotions are engendered and consciousness altered. Not infrequently there is a feeling of 'loss of self'—that is, a loss of the sense of separation—and a feeling of union with the other members of the congregation."[47]

Rituals have a mysterious way of overcoming our separation and creating a collective body. In fact, sociologist Emile Durkheim calls this "collective effervescence."[48] I find it easiest to think of effervescence as being like seltzer. Pour seltzer into a glass, and it excitedly pops and pops while small bubbles dance up to the surface together. As the seltzer sends bubbles rising up the glass, so also elated graduates toss their caps into the air as the audience rises with applause to joyfully celebrate them. This is collective effervescence.

Even the most serious rituals can bring us into this collective unity. When the uniformed officers surround the flag-draped casket, call commands, and take up and fold the flag to present it to the mourning family members, all stand in rapt attention for the twenty-one-gun salute and the playing of "Taps." Mourners grab the hands of their loved ones, and tears flow freely. Such rituals strengthen societal bonds.

A student recently informed me that anyone who has served in the military for any amount of time can have military honors.[49] It is interesting that even if an individual served in the military for only two of their eighty-five years of life, and even if they served in their early twenties, the military tells them they belong by offering them honors; they were and are part of something larger than themselves—the military community. Their boot-camp initiation ritual created a permanent bond.

Part of the power of military honors is the repetition of the ritual with little or no alteration. Certainly, rituals can be, and frequently are, altered or changed, but there is something about threads of familiarity that enhance ritual meaning. Some sort of Lenten fasting has been my habit since I became an adult, but this year my Lenten fasting was inconsistent and almost nonexistent. And then we came to Palm Sunday, and I had the same sense of anticipation, the same release of tension, the same feeling of "we're almost there" that I do every Holy Week. Easter still comes, regardless of the strength of my fasting. On Palm Sunday I paraded around the same church with the same people I parade with each year, and I felt the unifying power of the yearly ritual.

Not only does ritual bring us together; it socializes us. It tells us what is important to our community, who is who, how to become, and what we value. The simplest worship service does this. Through corporate song and action, we demonstrate our theology and values. The portions on which we spend the most time are the most important, and there are clear leaders and followers. A worship service with a baptism or confirmation demonstrates how to become. Ritual is "the means by which collective beliefs and ideals are simultaneously generated, experienced, and affirmed as real by the community."[50] Coming together like this unifies us with one another.

On Monday, September 10, 2001, I finished teaching Greek at 9:00 p.m. at our Worth Street campus, ten blocks north of the World Trade Center. When I returned from my run the next morning—a beautiful, sunny Tuesday—I turned on AM 880 to hear the day's weather and news. The first plane had hit the tower, and all our heartbeats stopped. I had been so close just a few hours before.

The next few days, churches were packed, and I returned to the city on Sunday to attend my full Midtown church. Many were looking to church ritual to help with their complex emotions and their sense of a loss of control and agency. They needed a structured performance that would take them to another world, if only for an hour. It was not only about theology; it was also about the fact that we turn to familiar rituals in times of deep mourning and great celebration. When we have experienced disintegration, we go to a place whose rituals unite. We want to be united with Christ and each other in the simplest meal of bread and wine. We need to *do something* because the complexity cannot be expressed simply with words or in thoughts but only by our bodies and with others. We hardly talked; we just looked at each other and shared a sense of knowing.

After church I headed down to Ground Zero, where the haze still filled the air. I walked across Worth Street, the closest civilians could get, and the silence there was deafening. No cars, no sirens, no talking. We clapped for each vehicle and person that entered or left the site. I saw makeshift memorials and missing-persons signs. Others had to do something too, and I was united with them and the country in collective mourning. Standing there and watching, the simplest of rituals, gave me a place and time for shock, sadness, and more. An act as simple as honoring those who were leaving gave me a sense of agency when my world was unmoored. Ritual united and ritual helped.

Right-Now Ritual: Lament

Two-thirds of the psalms are lament psalms; some are individual laments, and some are corporate. I often wonder how it might help and unite Christians to incorporate lament in our corporate worship services as the presence of lament psalms in the Psalter suggests we do. Lament psalms follow a basic three-part pattern or key progression:

Complaint: "This is wrong!"
Petition: "Help me, God!"
Declaration: "I trust you, God!"

Lament

Complaint: *Kneel down on the floor in body or in spirit and tell God what is wrong. Often, complex emotions feel like they knock us down; may they knock us down to our knees before a loving God. Hold your hands in front of you like a cup. Imagine putting what is wrong into your hands, away from your body.*
   Ask for Help: *When you have placed enough in your hands and feel ready, stand up with your hands still cupped in front of*

---

you. Ask God for help; you may even suggest how you think God might help.

Declaration: *Slowly lift your cupped hands above your head, declaring that you trust God to be with you in this grief and that you believe God to be faithful. Add other declarations of attributes of God that seem appropriate. Physically push what is in your hands above your head and away as you bring your arms wide in a half circle down to your sides.*

Still standing, cup your hands again in front of you in a receptive posture. Say, "I remain confident of this: I will see the goodness of the LORD in the land of the living. Wait for the LORD; be strong and take heart and wait for the LORD" (Ps. 27:13–14). Silently receive comfort and assurance from God. You may wish to finish with a prayer.[51]

With-Friends Ritual: After an Important Person Leaves

When a child leaves home or has an extended absence from home, parents and siblings feel significant loss. This move toward an "empty nest," however, is not the only loss of this type; when a close friend moves across the country to take a job, the loss is similar. Ritualizing this change helps people maintain connection (unity) with the person who left.

This ritual is intended to help those left behind process the loss when it is a positive move for the person who leaves (it can even be done to honor the person *as* he or she leaves). The key progression is naming the benefits of the relationship, naming the losses, declaring hope for a continuing relationship, and blessing.

After an Important Person Leaves

Preparation

Those who remain are invited to:

- Print a photo of the family or friends together and put it in a frame (ideally this photo would be taken at the time of leaving).
- Write down the benefits that the friend or child has brought to those left behind in two categories: first, the ones that continue and second, the ones that cannot continue due to the distance. The type that cannot continue might be something like meeting for coffee on short notice at a favorite café or chatting at the water cooler.
- Purchase three types of candles: one large three-wick one and multiple votives and tea lights. The number of votives should correspond to the number of items on the list of benefits that will continue, and the number of tea lights should correspond to the number of items on the list of those that will not continue.
- Invite friends to the ritual and explain their role as witnesses; ask one to be the leader who will pray the opening prayer and do the closing blessing.

The Ritual

Set the three-wick candle in the middle of a table. Surround it with a circle of votives, and surround that with the tea lights.

Begin with prayer. Leader opens the ritual with a prayer that invites God's presence and blesses the action about to take place. She or he will then light one of the wicks of the three-wick candle, stating, "This wick symbolizes the light of (name of person who left) in the lives of (names of the people who remain)."

Those who remain name the benefits of the person that will continue, and for each one, they light a votive candle using the flame that represents the person who left.

In a similar way, they light the tea lights and name the benefits lost due to distance.

When ready to let go (this process should not be rushed), those who remain will blow out all but one of the tea lights, stating, "I will miss (name of person who left), and I will miss what we will no longer share."

Those who remain will use the final tea light to light the two other wicks of the three-wick candle, stating, "While I miss (name of person who left), I still hope for their light in my life to grow and remain strong in new ways." *They may speak any other hope that they have.*

Leader closes the ritual with this blessing: Even as life brings change to the relationships, you will always be (state relationship—e.g., the mother) of (name of person who left). May God give you joy as you savor the benefits of this person in your life. May God grant you strength to grieve the loss of their presence, and "may the God of hope fill you with all joy and peace as you trust in him, so that you may overflow with hope by the power of the Holy Spirit" (Rom. 15:13). Amen!

Those who remain may keep the three-wick candle and photo together in a special place; when they light it, they remember the ritual along with the relationship's benefits, the loss of those benefits, and the hope they have.

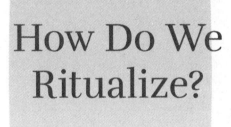

PART TWO

How Do We Ritualize?

4

Avoiding Powerless Rituals

Ritual "Don'ts"

I HOPE YOU ARE CONVINCED OF THE POWER OF RITUAL, the theme of part 1 of this book. Even so, not all rituals tap into the power. Not all ritual is dead ritual, but some rituals do, in fact, seem dead. According to the prophet Amos, the life-giving nature of the prescribed rituals does not come only from following commanded ritual actions. It is more holistic.

Therefore this is what the Lord, the LORD God Almighty, says . . .

> "I hate, I despise your religious festivals;
>   your assemblies are a stench to me.
> Even though you bring me burnt offerings and grain
>   offerings,
>   I will not accept them.
> Though you bring choice fellowship offerings,
>   I will have no regard for them.
> Away with the noise of your songs!
>   I will not listen to the music of your harps.

But let justice roll on like a river,
righteousness like a never-failing stream!" (Amos
5:16, 21–24)

Amos declares that the Israelites practice powerless rituals that are unacceptable to God. They follow the commanded ritual patterns given in Exodus and Leviticus; they sacrifice the animals, fast, and sing. But without justice, these rituals are powerless; they do not reconcile the people to God, "because their worship is accompanied by unfair taxes on the poor, corruption, and the oppression of the vulnerable."[1] Rituals do not always work; they do not always do what they are intended to do.

Some say we should therefore rid ourselves of rituals, but of course, that would be impossible. It does not fix the problem, because the problem was not that they did the rituals. The problem was the *way* they did them. God calls the Israelites to do not just the rituals but *all* the law—rituals *and* justice. We need not get rid of the former and do only the latter. We do both.

These are Paul's words to the Corinthians:

In the following directives I have no praise for you, for your meetings do more harm than good. In the first place, I hear that when you come together as a church, there are divisions among you, and to some extent I believe it. No doubt there have to be differences among you to show which of you have God's approval. So then, when you come together, it is not the Lord's Supper you eat, for when you are eating, some of you go ahead with your own private suppers. As a result, one person remains hungry and another gets drunk. Don't you have homes to eat and drink in? Or do you despise the church of God by humiliating those who have nothing? What shall I say to you? Shall I praise you? Certainly not in this matter! (1 Cor. 11:17–22)

The Corinthians shared the ritual of the Lord's Supper, but they did so according to social stratification. Because the rich Christians' houses were larger and their lifestyle more leisurely, they hosted and began the meal before the poor came. Some even ate their own individual suppers. Amy Peeler writes, "Paul's concern seems not to be only with rampant individuality but also inequality."[2] Their individuality and lack of unity and care for one another made the supper they ate not the Lord's Supper; it made the ritual powerless.[3] Christians don't interpret this passage to mean that we should therefore stop sharing the Lord's Supper. We share the Lord's Supper *and* work on unity and care for one another.

This second part of the book will teach you how to create rituals that are powerful and transformative and that will help you process things that are hard and deep. I will provide tools that will help us avoid powerless and empty rituals and create rituals that communicate meaning and stay in our memory for the rest of our lives. This chapter begins with the fundamentals of divine and human work in rituals as well as assumptions I make about Christian ritualizers. Then we will observe several pitfalls to avoid.

The Divine and the Human in Rituals

Many hesitate to think about measuring the transformational power (or lack thereof) of rituals from culture or religion. Is it really okay to choose a paradigm of ritual potency and hold it up as a measuring stick to rituals? Anthropologists and ritual theorists tend toward description: this is what these rituals do, and this is how they do it. They shy away from evaluation: this worked, but this did not work. Very few engage in ritual criticism. Officially, we seldom evaluate rituals.

Unofficially, we do it all the time.

"I loved how they recessed to 'Signed, Sealed, Delivered'—it made me so happy!"

"The singing was too long and repetitive."

"Calvin would disagree with that theology."

"Did she really spend forty-five minutes on just one word in that one verse?"

"The Bible came alive to me when they read it together that way!"

Whether the comments are positive or negative, all are a type of criticism of ritual. Ronald Grimes puts it this way: "Scholars who deny the element of criticism implicit in both the study and the practice of ritual are like Pentecostals who deny they engage in ritual even though their spontaneous actions are stylized and predictable."[4] Even if our criticism is implicit, we still engage in it.

One might object and say we should learn not to do it. After all, in Christian rituals like corporate worship or baptism, God is working. We do not get to evaluate whether God worked or not. Christian rituals are not about us and whether we think they do what they say they do. God decides. Episcopal priest Susan Marie Smith calls God's work in Christian rituals "doctrinal efficacy." "I now pronounce you husband and wife" or "What God has joined together, let no one separate" (Mark 10:9) are declarations of God's work: the ritual does what it says.[5] The baptized are transformed; the people receive the body and blood of Christ; God works, and we do not evaluate God's work.

I hope you are objecting here, if only a little. What about us? What about our subjective experience of the ritual and its results in our lives? We all know people who were baptized as infants and have lived a fruitful Christian life. Yet we also know others who were baptized as infants and now want nothing to do with the Christian God. Did God work?

This question is profound and deserves theological reflection. For our purposes, however, suffice it to say that several ancient theologians saw God's work interacting with human reception or experience in Christian rituals. Smith calls human experience "operational efficacy" and, beginning with Augustine, shows that both God's work and human experience are at play in the efficacy, or transformational power, of rituals.[6] In essence, we can *believe and declare* God's work in a ritual, but we also can (and sometimes do not) *experience* God's work in a ritual.

In this chapter and the next, our evaluation of the power of certain rituals will focus on the human experience of the work of God in a ritual. There are things we can do in preparing for and performing a ritual that enhance or detract from our experience of it.

I need to describe ritual as performance again. I mentioned earlier that when I use the word I'm not talking about fake or self-aggrandizing behavior. Right now I'm talking about how we do things. In rituals the primary goal of the performance is to enhance the experience of the participant. If I lack confidence, the participant will lose interest; if I stumble over the Bible reading, it will harm the participant's experience; if I am unprepared, the participant will not be able to follow the story.[7]

Though our rituals may come from God, and though God acts in them, they "are also constructed by human beings and therefore imperfect. . . . However sacred, rites are not beyond the ken of mortals. Therefore, they are subject to ongoing assessment. They can be judged wanting. They can be improved upon. They can fail."[8] Ritual criticism acknowledges ritual imperfection and identifies paths for ritual improvement.

We are about to explore general practices that seem to make transformational rituals successful as well as practices to avoid. Those practices will focus not on what God does in ritual but rather on what the performers and participants do. God acts in God's way according to God's desires. God can break in and change what we do at any moment.

When I was a kid, my dad repaired our cars. He would be on a flattened cardboard box under the car, and I would sit by the toolbox, handing him the tools he requested. Sometimes I handed him the wrong tool, but as I learned which was which, I helped him better. At one point I graduated to changing the tires and the oil. My dad certainly did not need me, but he wanted me there, and I helped him do the work. So it is with God. God does the work under the car, so to speak, but we are involved. These chapters help us be involved in such a way that we work alongside God and our work enhances the participant experience.

Some Preliminary Assumptions

Part 1 of this book elaborated on two primary ideas. First, we are human ritualizers. We invent rituals all the time. Second, ritual is powerful and useful. Ritual transforms, embodies, helps, and unites. For the most part we have explored all this as positive, but now I make a clear disclaimer: ritualizing can transform people negatively. We saw this with Kody Scott's initiation into the Crips, but negative transformation can be more subtle. Let us not naively assume that our Christian identity will prevent us from forming people negatively through ritual. We must take care. So, as I continue, I want to clarify basic assumptions I make regarding you, the ritualizer, and those with whom you might create or perform rituals. I assume you are Christian, ethical, and not working alone.[9]

When I assume you are Christian, I assume you understand God, the Trinity, salvation, the Bible, and the church. Certainly we all have differing levels of this understanding; I do not expect you to teach theology as I do. What matters is that you are a believer who has enough understanding to have faith specifically in the Christian God. Your identity as a believer is important because it is not a Bible verse or a prayer that necessarily makes a ritual properly Christian. Christian rituals are done by Christians. Some of my personal rituals do not have overt biblical references or prayers, but as a Christian, I do it all in the sight of God. Because God has made me sacred, what I do is sacred; my rituals have sacramental potentiality that is activated by faith. Because I am a Christian, God is always there. Ritualizers with a deep understanding of Christianity will create the most transformational *Christian* rituals.

I assume not only that you understand Christianity but also that you live it out. You worship individually and corporately, you seek spiritual formation, and your actions follow biblical commands and parallel those of Jesus. Because the power of ritual is great, ethical rituals must be created by ethical people.

Third, I assume you do not do this alone. Certainly, the right-now rituals of this book are often practiced individually, but all are practiced and edited by others before they come to you. Rituals unite people not only as they are enacted but also in their creation. Below I will say more about requiring much from the community and avoiding individualizing.

I want to share one final thought before we look at ritual don'ts: you can make existing rituals more powerful and life-changing. Ritual invention can be a long and arduous process; it is often easier to take what already exists and use the hints below to increase the rituals' transformational power.

Ritual Don'ts

Don't Use Only Words

We all know that the adage "Sticks and stones will break my bones, but words will never hurt me" is utterly untrue. Words are powerful. Words curse and bless. Words and the tone with which they are stated carry deep meaning.

But rituals are so much more than words.

Maybe this is already clear. When we think of a beautiful and moving wedding ritual, it is so much more than words. The rings, the special clothing, movements such as the recessional, the planning, the people present—all of this is party to the wedding's powerful transformation. A wedding uses so much more than words.

It seems, however, that popular books of Christian rituals include only words. I enjoy Douglas McKelvey's popular two-volume work *Every Moment Holy*.[10] He writes liturgies for almost any occasion, and his words are inspirational and helpful for various times in life. The liturgies are for both individuals and groups and are good theological and practical words. However, they lack symbols and rubrics.

For liturgists and ritualists, rubrics are instructions for the actions that are to be performed when we say the words. All books of liturgies have them. They tell the minister what to do with the water, bread, and wine and when to invite congregants to kneel or process or pass the peace.

I mentioned the prayer of St. Ephrem in chapter 1, on embodiment. Here is the prayer:

O Lord and Master of my life, deliver me from sloth, faintheartedness, lust of power and idle talk. Grant rather the spirit of chastity, humility, patience, and love to your servant. Yea, Lord and King, grant me to see my own sin and not to judge my brother or sister, for thou art blessed now and ever and unto ages of ages.[11]

It is truly a beautiful prayer of repentance full of powerful words. Consider the same prayer with rubrics:

"O Lord and Master of my life, deliver me from sloth, faintheartedness, lust of power and idle talk." *Cross yourself, lie flat on your face before God, and then rise.*

"Grant rather the spirit of chastity, humility, patience, and love to your servant." *Cross yourself, lie flat on your face before God, and then rise.*

"Yea, Lord and King, grant me to see my own sin and not to judge my brother or sister, for thou art blessed now and ever and unto ages of ages." *Cross yourself, lie flat on your face before God, and then rise.*

Yes, the words are powerful. Joined with the prostrations, however, they unify, humble, and transform. The rubrics direct our actions.

The rubrics in the (Episcopalian) Book of Common Prayer are not complete. For example, the Ash Wednesday service simply states, "*The ashes are imposed with the following words:* 'Remember you are dust, and to dust you shall return.'"[12] If someone who is unfamiliar with the service reads these instructions, they are left with many questions, including, Where does one impose the ashes? Does one just make a dot with them? And what kind of ashes are used?

One of the first times our college had an Ash Wednesday service, we retrieved ashes from a fireplace and imposed them on people's foreheads. Bad idea. We quickly found that fireplace ashes are clumpy and do not stick to foreheads; they mostly make a mess of clothing, the table, and the floor. Proper Ash Wednesday ashes are the burnt palm fronds from the previous year's Palm Sunday. The church purchases them. They are fine, not clumpy, and very black. They stick to foreheads when imposed in the sign of the cross.

The Book of Common Prayer rubrics are not enough for the uninitiated. Much is learned only through experience. The Ash Wednesday service also has the rubric "The Peace is then exchanged." The rubric does not direct the minister to state, "The peace of the Lord be always with you," or the congregants to respond, "And also with you." It also does not direct the congregants to say similar words to one another with a handshake or a hug. Having experienced this ritual before, however, ministers know to lift their hands to the congregants, bless them with the words of the peace, and invite them to greet one another.

Rituals are so much more than words.

Don't Fantasize, Mythologize, or Borrow Wholesale

The following recommendations are based on mistakes people make when planning rites of passage. They are broad enough, however, to apply to any ritual outside of our own context that we want to perform. Let me explain with a rite of passage example.

In *Healing the Masculine Soul*, Gordon Dalbey describes a Nigerian rite of passage for males. In that locale, boys live with their mother while their father lives by himself in another hut. When the boy is about twelve, it is time for the ritual. The boy's father appears with a masked *nmoo* (person who represents a spirit) and a drummer close to the boy's hut that he shares with his mother. The drummer plays, and the *nmoo* dances, both actions working together to claim the area in front of the hut for the men. When the *nmoo* signals, the drumming changes, and the *nmoo* bangs on the hut's door over and over until the mother appears, shielding her son. The boy's father and the company of men call, "Come out, son of my people, come out!" The mother refuses and slams the door. So goes the drama over and over: the *nmoo* dances, the drummer drums, the men call, and the mother refuses. Finally, the boy breaks out and is led with other boys to a place in the forest to learn the ways of men and to be transformed.[13]

Dalbey imagines a similar rite of passage in his North American Christian context. The men worship together at the church to strengthen themselves, and then they go as a group to each house to pick up the boys. They sing hymns on the lawn while the minister calls for the boy and the mother refuses. When the boy breaks free, they go together to a campground, where the boys are instructed. The final rite is a laying on of hands with prayer for the Holy Spirit, as in the traditional sacrament of confirmation.[14]

Dalbey's dream of a rite of passage is well intentioned. His list of learning goals is impressive and would take much longer than a weekend or even two weeks at the campground to accomplish. Some parts are a bit odd, however. If a group of men from the church were to show up on our lawn, singing hymns and calling for my son while I refused, the neighbors might call the police. Dalbey's dream contains some of what Grimes calls fantasizing, mythologizing, and wholesale borrowing.

When Dalbey was in Nigeria and heard about the ritual, he was mesmerized and wanted it for boys in his church. He might have thought, "If they have this, they will never question their manhood, and it will transform them into strong men!" When we have special experiences in foreign contexts, we often fantasize and exaggerate the other culture's greatness or depravity. Elsewhere I have written about Grimes's insight on this point:

> Grimes writes, "Rites of passage can seem perfectly magical— but only if you keep your eyes and ears trained on what transpires center stage. Backstage, there often seethes a morass of spiritual stress and social conflict." The pictures may say a thousand words, but another few thousand are locked up behind the scenes because they are not quite as picturesque. Humans enact rites. Humans in families enact rites. Humans who identify themselves with certain institutions enact rites. Given the sometimes fragile, often volatile, always complex relationships between humans, it is only natural to assume there is more than meets the eye. Rites of passage are deeply human experiences and the limits of humanity affect them. "Actual rites are local and specific, usually more ordinary and less dramatic than much of the popular literature would lead us to believe. Real initiation rites are characterized by boredom, spending money, family squabbles, and lots of tedious labor."[15]

While a ritual may look and be amazing, what we see is not the whole story. And simply because it seems to work in one culture does not mean it should be imported mostly "as is" to another culture. Rituals are tied to culture.

Sometimes it is the words that are culturally determined. I used to babysit the son of a namer. Her job was to name corporations and products in such a way that they would function well across cultures. Since sometimes words and their meaning vary between cultures, we need to be careful with words and names.

It is usually the nonverbal aspects, however, that are culturally determined. In the above example, while drumming, dancing, and singing outside may be perfectly normal in an African tribal culture, singing on the lawn would be rather odd where I live. It is best to connect rituals with local traditions rather than borrow a culturally distant ritual wholesale while fantasizing about its great power.

While few of us may have traveled to Africa, many of us experience rituals from other cultures. Perhaps it is a Jewish wedding, a Buddhist funeral, or a ritual from a different Christian tradition. As an intentional ritualizer, I sometimes think, "That part of the ritual was so amazing. I want to do it in mine!" This may have been what Dalbey thought about breaking the boys away from their mothers.

Dalbey noticed the different god of the Nigerian rite, but he seems to have overlooked some cultural differences, at least for the initial ritual. The Nigerian rite of passage goes back generations and is based in a communal, patriarchal culture with little individual choice. Dalbey and I share a Western culture that is often patriarchal in a different way, is not communal, and prizes individual choice. The church is a subculture that sometimes agrees with the broader culture and sometimes disagrees with it but is always influenced by it. The calling out of the boy needs to be done in a manner that better befits the local culture, and the boy needs some prior understanding of what might happen so he can choose. The boys in Nigeria had watched this ritual happen for their whole lives, and every man had taken part in it.[16]

Our rituals must avoid fantasizing and borrowing. In addition, we should avoid mythologizing, which is reading about a ritual in a novel or watching it in a movie and thinking we can do it.[17] Movies and books are the stuff of myth—fiction that is beautiful to behold but is nevertheless not reality. We can easily identify Frodo's transformative rite of passage in *The Lord of the Rings* as myth. After all, he is a hobbit living in a world of magic, embarking on a rite of passage quest. It is more difficult to identify ritual fiction as myth when the actors are human and in a world like ours. Still, we must remind ourselves that what we read and see in movies is myth, not reality. Let us not fantasize, mythologize, or borrow wholesale.

Don't Individualize

This warning is particularly important for Western ritualizers. Rituals are best when connected to community. Some elope to avoid controlling parents and everything that goes along with planning a wedding. Their disappointed community often later throws a reception for them because a wedding is not just about two people. It is also about their community.

My husband is from a culture where engagement is not an agreement between two people; it is an agreement (and commitment) between two families. It takes time and planning, and the families are present for the "ask." My Western sensibility found this both beautiful and annoying at the same time.

Orthodox Christian priests in Middle Eastern communal cultures do a betrothal ceremony at the engagement. In North American culture, the Orthodox betrothal is performed at the same time as the wedding, presumably because North Americans break engagements more often. Since betrothal binds the two together, a broken engagement requires a priest to break the bond. This leads us to a tentative conclusion that a communal engagement transforms two people into one more effectively than a Western, individualized one that is an agreement between only two people.

Now, I am not saying that a man needs to get down on one knee in the presence of Mom and Dad while the woman stands across the room with her sisters surrounding her. We have our own recognizable rituals, and we can keep them. It is simply good to keep in mind that individualized rituals are less transformative than communal ones. Individualizing is best avoided.

. . . .

My students evaluate each course I teach. When I receive the evaluations in an email after the semester, I have a familiar feeling in my gut. It is a combination of anxiety and anticipation—but mostly anxiety. I tend toward overachieving perfectionism, and one negative comment on one evaluation can make me judge myself a failure. So, I have a rule: I am allowed to read through them only once, and I must try to remember the positive comments (I remember the negative ones with no effort).

I teach worship and theology; some of my courses are fully online with recorded lectures. Two students at different times have stated I sound like a valley girl and am annoying in my recordings. I could have chosen to ignore these comments, chalking them up to grumpiness. Hundreds of other students have no such critique. Instead, what I did was practice modulating my voice so that all my students would find me easy to listen to. The teaching about worship and theology remained, but the presentation made for an easier reception. We can draw an analogy between this practice and Christian ritual. God's work is like the teaching; it is there regardless of the details of the presentation. And the little details of the ritual are like the modulation of my voice; we can tweak how we do things to give our communities an easier time understanding and participating in the ritual. This is the goal of critique.

We have an opportunity both to invent rituals and to revise the ones we have. We can evaluate our rituals according to whether we practice the ritual "don'ts" described above, and then we can make changes to increase the rituals' power. This is an exciting process!

Right-Now Ritual: Letting Go of Powerless Rituals

Perhaps reading this chapter has revealed something lacking in a ritual you love. We are often very attached to our rituals, personal and communal, even though they may be judged wanting. Ritualizing is human, and changing rituals involves loss. In order to positively move forward, then, this right-now ritual helps us let go of the ineffective elements of a beloved ritual. It also opens us up to the creative act of renewing the ritual. This is best done when one has already judged a ritual ineffective. While we may be tempted to do it for many rituals at once, it will be most effective if it is done for each ritual. If the renewal is for a personal ritual, this can be done alone; if it is for a communal one, it will be most effective if done with others. The key progression is letting go and preparing to receive.

Letting Go of Powerless Rituals

Hold your hands in front of you, palms up, in a receptive posture.
Lord, thank you for all (identify the ritual) has given to (me/us). (*Describe how it has helped.*) I am grateful for what I have received.
Turn your hands palm down as if to release.
Certain parts of the ritual are no longer effective, so I let go of (*describe what is ineffective about the ritual, such as excessive individualization*).

Turn hands palm up again to receive.

As I have let go of what is ineffective, God, I ask you to show me how to work better with your creative work and make the experience more effective. Give (me/us) wisdom, clarity, and Holy Spirit inspiration for the change. I am excited and ready to receive what you have for me. Amen.

5

Pursuing Powerful Rituals

"WOMAN WAS ONE OF THE MOST fulfilling, life-changing periods of my life."

"*Woman* transformed me by helping me find my voice."

"The *Woman* program really just gave me permission to dream again. There was a beautiful mingling of heaven and earth that took place when a roomful of women who passionately love the Lord began to rise up and take their place in the kingdom of God."

"I learned that my cleats did not need to be replaced with heels because both were comfortable. My jersey was just as mesmerizing as any dress. My brain was a gift, not a turn-off, and respect was earned regardless of my gender."

"The result of this year discovering who I am as a woman has been a complete release of every lie that I believed—that I wasn't enough or that I didn't deserve happiness. I've been able to find my identity in God, and because of that I know that I am more than enough, and that he made me exactly who I am with no mistakes. And to commemorate this season in my life, I got a tattoo. It's the word 'enough' and it's in the shape of a cross and I got it close to my foot because I want it to be my foundation that I walk in from here on out."

These are just some of the stories of the transformation wrought through *Woman*. There is a beautiful mystery to how God works uniquely in each participant. We simply do our best to partner with God's work. This partnering involves creating rituals with carefully chosen symbols and the four hallmarks of the most transformative and powerful rituals.

Carefully Chosen Symbols

I wear a plain gold band on my left ring finger. I first wore it on my right hand, because in my husband's tradition, both engaged persons get a ring and transfer it to their left hand at the wedding. I never take it off. It was blessed; it means unity and connection to my husband, and to the broader population, it means I am married. Were I to take it off and throw it at my husband, that act would be a breach of our connection and would probably lead to a break.

It is just a ring, fashioned by the apt hands of my brother-in-law in Athens, Greece. In another size or on another finger, throwing or losing the ring would have little consequence. As it is, in my size and worn on my left ring finger, having been blessed and placed there during a ritual, it has great consequence. That is how symbols work.

We began investigating symbols in chapter 3. I will add a few thoughts here because the most life-changing rituals have carefully chosen symbols, and the symbols are more than just objects; the who, how many, where, when, and why of rituals are also powerfully symbolic.

Ritual theorist Victor Turner sees symbols as the basic building blocks of rituals; one symbol does a lot more than one word or even many words. One symbolic object communicates multiple meanings, links disparate phenomena, and acts out human unity.[1] We cannot do all of this in one word, let alone in a homily or sermon. Symbols are powerful; Christians have historically believed there is power in water, bread, and wine.[2]

When Susan Marie Smith creates a pastoral rite, she first searches for a defining metaphor that is connected to the Christian narrative of salvation; this metaphor inspires the symbolic action that is the centerpiece of the ritual.[3] I am both a little ashamed and rather amused to admit that the symbol I first chose for *Woman* was a Wingding. Wingdings was a font in earlier versions of Microsoft Word. This font gave symbols for each letter, and I was partial to a symbol that looked like a budding flower. We were a poor start-up, and I made our "logo," despite my inexperience. I incorporated the Wingding into the logo and then took it to a jeweler in my hometown to have a solid-silver pendant made. It was great until PowerPoint created a template that used this wingding as a bullet point and some participants made the connection between the two. It was already our symbol, however, connected to the overarching metaphor of *Woman* and used in the central symbolic action of the Crossing Over Ceremony.

The metaphor for *Woman* is a journey. Women are at different places on the journey of womanhood as we develop our relationships with God, self, others, and creation. The purpose of the rite of passage is for women to begin and continue that journey as together we discover, engage, and empower. We focus on all this through the mini-journey of a year together. A budding flower is an apt symbol for this journey of life. It symbolizes many things—one being that we have begun the journey of womanhood and will continue to develop. The budding flower is visible on all printed and electronic materials for *Woman*. The central symbolic act of the Crossing Over Ceremony occurs when leaders and alumnae give participants a necklace with a solid-silver pendant bearing the symbol. The act is viscerally moving every time. When we began the second decade of *Woman*, we worked with a designer to change the symbol in such a way as to connect to the previous one but also be an original design. The overarching metaphor and its visual symbol are key to ritual power.

Symbolism is not limited to objects, however. Priya Parker has written insightfully on why and how people gather together. She references multiple types of gatherings, including church gatherings. Her primary suggestion for meaningful gathering is establishing the purpose. This purpose is similar to Smith's overarching metaphor in ritual. The metaphor is like an artistic picture of the purpose of the gathering. The "why" (purpose) precedes and forms the "how" of the ritual. Parker's work on gatherings is helpful here because rituals are a type of gathering. In fact, she has an entire chapter called "Create a Temporary Alternative World," an idea we discussed in chapter 3.

Parker delineates the importance of "who," "how many," and "where" for gatherings. Who is invited, how many are invited, and the location of the ritual are important symbols because they speak without words. Let me apply her principles to a mistake we made with *Woman* and how we corrected it. We had twenty-six participants one year. This was so many people that we could not maintain properly deep personal relationships and accountability—two of our values—at the regular meetings that took place between the initiation and the Crossing Over. Parker writes that as a group number approaches thirty, it begins to feel like a party and is therefore too big for single conversations.[4] In *Woman*, if our leadership team and venue were larger, we could have accommodated more participants and strategized to maintain our values. Parker states that groups of six are conducive to intimacy and groups of twelve to fifteen allow for diversity and a little mystery.[5] We decided to cap *Woman* at twenty-one participants. They could divide into groups of seven plus one leader to begin the regular meeting and could also meet in groups of three seated at the café tables.

The number of people in a group is a powerful symbol that shapes how individuals act. In *Woman*'s small groups of three and seven, the participants created personal relationships and could not hide. While the whole group together had a festive feel, we still created space for personal conversations.

Not all rituals will have regular meetings like *Woman*, however. Many will be a onetime event where numbers and those invited are decided according to the purpose. The *Woman* initiation includes only leaders, participants, and the mentors they choose; it is a female-only event. Thus, we begin the journey with a small group of those who will be active together for the next seven months. The Crossing Over, however, is a party, and men are invited. It is formal, and those present are leaders, participants, mentors, and two to four invitees for each participant. The larger but still limited number and the formal paper invitations signal the type and importance of the gathering. "Who" and "how many" are important symbols that speak without words.

In *Woman*, our numbers were constrained by the venue available to us. Parker suggests choosing a location according to the purpose or overarching metaphor for the rite.[6] The initiation and the Crossing Over Ceremony differed in size, but it was important to begin and complete this journey together in the same place. This repetition of venue would inspire memories of the start of the journey and intuitively create meaning.

Parker suggests that, at times, reconfiguring a room is enough to make it suitable for the purpose.[7] In our case the initiation had a formal reception with tables to fill up the space. The Crossing Over had something more like a cocktail reception in the adjoining room so that the greater number of participants could fit in the venue itself. Also, the room was Presidents' Hall, a beautifully formal room in a mansion, and the walls were adorned with all the (male) presidents of the college. At first, we carefully removed the images, as we felt they gazed with disapproval. When we were no longer allowed to remove them, we incorporated them into the event, stating that they looked at us with joy, particularly the egalitarian founder. As we could not change the venue completely, we used it for our purposes, remembering that symbols are transformed by the way they are used. Parker writes, "A deft gatherer picks a place that elicits the behaviors she wants and plays down the behaviors she doesn't."[8]

"Who," "how many," and "where" embody the purpose of the ritual and provide important symbolic signals as to the part those gathered will play. Physical objects also display symbolic power. Engaged couples know this. They spend time and money choosing symbolic garments for their wedding ritual as well as paper invitations, a curated guest list, and a venue. The most transformative and powerful rituals center on an overarching metaphor or purpose as well as a symbolic act.

Four Hallmarks of a Powerful Ritual

Ronald Grimes believes that powerful rituals lodge themselves deeply in our being. He writes, "[Powerful] rites depend on inheriting, discovering, or inventing value-laden images that are driven deeply, by repeated practice and performance, into the marrow."[9] For Western culture, weddings and graduations are cultural rituals enriched by value-laden images that create meaning. Children watch, learn, and look forward to being the "stars" in these rituals. Powerful rituals often take their residence deep in us at an early age.

Grimes's three hallmarks of powerful rituals are based primarily on his observations of what makes a rite of passage seem to work. He observed many rites of passage, asked questions, and loosely (without a rubric or specific criteria) evaluated how well the rites worked. He noted that the more transformative ones had three hallmarks that correlated to their degree of potency. Grimes states that effective rituals *function* as attention-givers, have the *purpose* of transformation, and *require* much from individuals and their communities.[10] There is a fourth hallmark implicit in his work: effective rituals are repeated. Although not all rituals are rites of passage, Grimes's three hallmarks can be applied to a more general pursuit of transformative rituals. We can even apply these hallmarks to our corporate worship gatherings. I used Grimes's hallmarks to create *Woman*; I will demonstrate how they guided my decisions and how they can be used to guide the creation and enactment of rituals.

Powerful Rituals Function as Attention-Givers

We begin the *Woman* initiation with leaders and mentors telling their stories of when they truly understood themselves as Christian women. The stories vary. For one person the moment came when she gave birth, for another the understanding came gradually, and for one alumna of the program, that sense came through *Woman*. Aside from the alumnae, none tell a story of a ritualized passage. Most tell the story of looking back on an event years later and realizing, "Oh, yes—that was transformative for me." We often look back and realize transformation has happened.

Seldom, however, do we pay attention to formative events when they occur unless they are ritualized. Our churches and culture pay attention to graduations, weddings, and funerals, but there is not much in between. Sometimes a milestone birthday or a work promotion is celebrated, but it varies from person to person. Many cultures have rites of passage that pay attention to and mark the point when boys and girls become adults. Western cultures, however, do not generally honor adolescent rites of passage. This lack of rites of passage results in peer-driven initiations that are negative, such as sexual intercourse or, in the case of Kody Scott, gang initiation. Where there is no peer initiation, young people may experience continued confusion as to whether they are a child or an adult. With this in mind, Grimes is right when he says, "Unattended passages become spiritual sinkholes around which hungry ghosts, those greedy personifications of unfinished business, hover."[11]

His thoughts on rites of passage correlate easily with the psychological idea that ritual gives us aesthetic distance from an event and allows us an opportunity to process emotions that are too big or conflicting to pay attention to without a ritual. Admittedly, it is easier to ritualize events that seem positive. We want to suppress the negative. I have heard it said, however, that not paying attention to or suppressing negative events is like trying to hold a beach ball under the water. Sure, we can do it for a time, but it will come up eventually, usually strong and fast and uncontrolled. The beach ball usually hits us in the face. Ritual *functions* as an opportunity for us to pay attention to all of life.

Protestants can learn from the Messianic Jewish practice of the Mourner's Kaddish, as it allows participants to mark the losses due to death they experienced in the last year. We can also learn from the Orthodox Christian practice of mourning, in which they periodically come together and commemorate the deceased. Forty days after and again a year after the death, short services are appended onto the Sunday worship to remember the loved one. Following that, mourners can do the same small service any time the grief is overwhelming, usually each year on the anniversary of the death. After each such service, regardless of how many years it has been since the death, all parishioners greet the bereaved with "I am sorry for your loss" and "Christ is risen!" Thus, mourners have the opportunity to pay attention to their own loss and invite the body of believers to pay attention with them. I watched a woman weep at the ten-year memorial of her father. The ritual gave her the safe, contained opportunity to remember and mourn. Protestants need not agree with Orthodox Christian theology to see that this ritual practice is valuable.

Woman helps us pay attention to the passage into womanhood spiritually, psychologically, socially, emotionally, and in all other ways we can muster. Together we think, talk, and experience the journey of womanhood, and we walk forward together. Our consideration lasts a whole year—a whole year of paying attention to becoming a woman.

Most rituals will not be a yearlong rite of passage. Our Sunday corporate worship allows us to pay attention to God's work in the world and to respond to God. It is only in some branches of Protestantism that paying attention to God's work is not centered on the symbolic act of distributing and receiving bread and wine. With this centrality the metaphor and purpose are clearly centered in the paschal mystery. Weekly corporate worship is a time to pay attention to the work of God in history and the work of God in our personal and corporate lives.

Powerful Rituals Have the Purpose of Transformation

In the *Woman* rite of passage, we spend time paying attention to one portion of Christian discipleship: becoming a Christian woman. Because the purpose is relatively narrow, measuring transformation is easy; we can use the differences between the intake and exit surveys. Many other rituals will transform slowly and will be less easily measured. Nonetheless, don't we all desire transformation as we walk this journey of the Christian life?

I was the first one to the long white altar at Delta Lake Bible Camp when a speaker preached on being filled with the Holy Spirit. I wanted transformation, and I ran for it. Though more than thirty years have passed since that moment, I can still picture the place. The ritual of the altar call is meant to mark personal transformation that occurs in response to the word and presence of God. Response can be a clearly transformative moment, as it was for me, but response can also be holding out hands weekly to receive the body and blood as the act and elements transform individuals from the inside. The most powerful rituals have the *purpose* of transformation during the ritual; participants become different and then act differently in the world.

The transformation is significant; Grimes highlights the irrevocability of the change that a rite of passage acknowledges or achieves.[12] There is no going back: the caterpillar has become a butterfly. Tom Faw Driver agrees, stating, "Rituals are primarily instruments designed to change a situation: They are more like washing machines than books. A book may be *about* washing, but the machine takes in dirty clothes, and, if all goes well, transforms them into cleaner ones."[13] In *Woman*, participants are transformed into Christian women in their own perspective as well as in the broader community's perspective.

Grimes compares this to theater and considers the work of performance theorist Richard Schechner. "When a performance is efficacious, Schechner calls it a 'trans-formance,' because its work is to transform."[14] When I was mesmerized by *Sarafina!* on Broadway, the performance was a trans-formance, and I want that experience again. Good movies also have a way of taking me away and bringing me back changed.

Transformation is not easy to achieve, however. Gatherings that are not everything to everyone, ones that take a stand and are willing to unsettle guests, are the kind of gatherings that transform.[15] Even though *Woman* participants have prepared to be part of the program, they are uniformly nervous as they walk in for the initiation. Most come from free-church backgrounds and are unfamiliar with the formality of the ritual, even though it simply follows a format, is not completely extemporaneous, and incorporates symbolic action. While we do our best to help them feel honored and relaxed enough to participate, we make no apologies for unsettling them a little and taking a stand. In fact, part of becoming a Christian woman is employing confidence to stand and speak out, even when doing so will not please everyone.[16]

Parker states that we often confuse category with purpose: "The purpose of your church's small group was to allow church members to meet in smaller groups."[17] The more granular and specific the gathering's purpose, the easier it is to choose who, how many, and where. If the small group's purpose is to understand Romans, then it will be larger, need an expert, take place in a classroom, and be primarily for adults. If its purpose, however, is to bond families together on the journey of Christianity, it will be smaller than fifteen adults, need a facilitator, take place in a home, and include families.

Generally, a Christian wedding's purpose is to transform two Christians into one flesh in the presence of witnesses. This is God's work, but our performance can enhance the subjective experience of all present. Sometimes a wedding's overall purpose takes a back seat to favors, dresses, the guest list, social pressure, cost, and commercialism. A specific purpose gives us boundaries for who, how many, and all other portions of the ritual.[18]

Because *Woman* involves multiple meetings and rituals, it has many facets within the overall purpose of transforming girls into Christian women. We believe that reading, mentoring, conversing, bonding, reciting the *Woman* Affirmation of Identity, receiving blessing and prayer, creating a project that defines Christian womanhood, and participating in other activities facilitate transformation. The transformation, however, is most clearly experienced in the Crossing Over Ceremony, when symbols speak and act alongside participants, leaders, and God. It is then that, as the one participant said, "something changes in the air" for the women who walk out transformed, wearing a new necklace.

Parker warns us, in her chapter called "Don't Be a Chill Host," that transformation does not happen automatically. While a host (or worship/ritual leader) need not be controlling, one cannot assume that transformation will simply happen without help.[19] Several of her suggestions are apropos to creating transformative rituals: protect your guests (or participants), equalize them, and connect them.[20] Participants need protection from chatty Cathy and dramatic Uncle Joe, from boredom, and from their addictive cell phones. If we want to bring Janice the CEO and Chad the construction worker together as the body of Christ, we need to equalize them as sister and brother and to connect them on the grounds of both having five-year-old boys. This will not happen on its own.

When *Woman* brings honors students, athletes, and HEOP[21] students together, we are intentional about equalizing and connecting them so that they form *communitas* ready to be transformed.[22] We require that they meet in groups of two or three outside of the regular meetings, and we give them opportunities to learn vulnerability and trust. *Communitas* increases the breadth of transformation available to each as they rejoice in one another's presentations at the Crossing Over.

Transformation may be the purpose of corporate worship, but it can be eclipsed by lighting and fashionable music, celebrity preaching, announcements, and more. A general idea of transformation is not enough; "love God, love people" needs more specificity. Church-year seasons lend themselves to specificity: the purpose of Lent, for example, is to transform worshipers through repentance. We should strive for the same degree of specificity in the transformative purposes of all our Christian rituals.

Powerful Rituals Require Much from Us

Before the initiation ceremony for *Woman*, participants have already filled out the intake survey, done an intake interview, arranged for a mentor, and paid a nonrefundable fee. Their investment of time and money is likely part of what makes the attrition rate for *Woman* so low. More than that, their initial and continuing investment tends to ensure active participation and increase transformation. Some balk at the requirements, but we make no apologies, because our purpose is transformation, and this is what it takes.[23]

We invest back. *Woman* mentors are adjuncts, professors, and staff members from the college community, and the leaders are members of that community as well as alumnae and others. The community connection aids in the transformation through both mentoring and leading. *Woman* has always been an intentionally diverse team effort that incorporates the community and uses the college's venue.

For the first several years of *Woman*, I simply assumed the participants adhered to *Woman* values and did the assigned work. After all, they had already invested, and if they were rule followers like me, they would do the work. I was wrong, and that became abundantly clear the same year our group was too big. So, we instituted a check-in form on which students affirm they completed the assignments for each meeting. When a participant does not complete all assignments, I go to her to find out why and whether everything is okay. If it is, I tell her that she needs to complete the work for that meeting as well as the next meeting's work before the next meeting. If she does not do the work, she is saying she no longer wants to be a part of *Woman*.

Perhaps you think I am too tough. But here's the thing: I am unwilling to compromise other participants' investment due to *one* participant's lack thereof. When a participant has not done the preparatory reading, she cannot fruitfully participate in the conversation, and that affects everyone. She may say something inaccurate or simply remain silent. Further, if she has not met with others in the group between meetings, *communitas* is compromised. Rituals are not only about individual participants. We have all experienced the awkward feeling when it becomes obvious that someone came to class unprepared.

Grimes writes that "ritual knowledge is rendered unforgettable only if it makes serious demands on individuals and communities, only if it is etched deeply into the marrow of soul and society."[24] Exceptions cannot be doled out to all or else the potency of the ritual will be compromised. I have found that people meet high bars. What leaders should do, then, is decide on requirements, communicate them, and keep them. We remember what we do, and we become what we practice. In between, we make choices as to where we will invest.

Parker places requirements for individuals and communities into the category of "pregame" or "pregathering." She writes that "90 percent of what makes a gathering effective is put in place beforehand."[25] Here Parker is not referencing the "who," "how many," "where," and "why." Those are important, yet those are all *things*; she sees the pregame as prepping *people*. Naming a gathering and having people *do* something rather than *bring* something are part of the pregame. They communicate what guests can expect and create a social contract between host and guest.[26]

One of my earliest adult attempts at a party was a complete flop. No one came. This was before cell phones and social media, and I just wanted to get people together. So, I invited several people I knew, assigned them either a savory or a sweet contribution, and waited for them to arrive at my apartment. My roommates and I consumed our contribution as the empty night wore on. I think people were a bit confused because it was not a birthday celebration, a Bible study, a game night, or a formal meal. The lack of purpose and name made the event too confusing to attract guests to my home. No pregame made no game.

In order to make its purpose clear, we named the rite of passage *Woman*, but the purpose of its individual gatherings is communicated in multiple ways. For the initiation, we use printed invitations that ask for semiformal attire. The style and request communicate what type of gathering it is. These aspects, in addition to the intake requirements, form the pre-game for *Woman*.

Not all pregames are created equal. Baby showers today often honor both mother and father, but the centerpiece is usually chatting and opening gifts. What if the purpose of a baby shower were a celebration of friendship and practical help for the to-be parents? What if the centerpiece were not the opening of gifts but some symbolic act inspired by the pregame? What if guests had a part to play that was different from simple gift giving? Some friends and I did something like this for a baby shower. Attendees sent photos of themselves with the mother-to-be and wrote a blessing for her new season. One of the hosts gathered them all into a small scrapbook, and at the shower we each read her our page. There was not a dry eye in the place. While the goal is not emotional expression, the tears displayed the power of the central symbolic act and highlighted female bonds and blessings.

We did not set out to require much from our community; this was simply one host's idea. I wonder how much more mean-ingful social gatherings might be if we were more intentional. Perhaps being intentional with the purpose or metaphor could help us pay attention and invest in ways that create transforma-tion, not just for the person honored but for all present. Once I finish this manuscript, I intend to have a completion party that coincides with the end of summer and the beginning of fall. It will be a variation on the at-church ritual at the end of this chapter. Guests will be invited to bring a symbol or photo of something they have completed this past year. At some point we will all show our symbols, state what we've finished, and toast the completion. This simple community participation in completion makes it meaningful.

Powerful Rituals Are Repeated

Implicit in Grimes's hallmarks is the repetition of rituals. They cannot lodge deeply in our marrow if they occur once in history. Wedding and graduation rituals are lodged in us because they are rituals that we repeatedly experience (whether for ourselves or others), and they have common actions and symbols. We know what they mean because we have experienced them, and we need not explain them with words.

Participants were transformed the first time we did *Woman*.[27] But later years had more transformative potential because the repetition lodged itself in the marrow of the Nyack College community. First-year students had heard about it from upper-year students and had dreamed about participating in it; faculty and staff served faithfully as mentors and invited others to join. Repetition did its work, increasing both the community investment and the attention paid to the passage. The symbolic necklace was widely recognized as identifying someone who had completed *Woman*. Repetition does not necessarily decrease meaning. It can, rather, increase it.

Consider the repetition in our churches of the Lord's Supper or Eucharist. Different Christian traditions disagree regarding how often this ritual should be repeated. Some think weekly repetition decreases its meaning, while others think weekly repetition gives it greater meaning. Most Protestant traditions celebrate the Lord's Supper at least once a month, so we all repeat the ritual. Jesus told us to.

I prefer a weekly (or even daily) Eucharist. I am happy to receive Christ frequently in a way that shows his unity as God and human and that gives me an opportunity to act as a person who is a unified whole. All my senses are engaged; I see, hear, touch, smell, and taste in a eucharistic service. I am reminded that I interact with the triune God not as a mind but as a body, and the ritual is a unique opportunity to act out this truth. The repetition of the action lodges its power deeply in my marrow.

The purpose of the Eucharist is transformation and unity. Paul writes to the Corinthians about its unifying character, and the early church thought it transformed us, allowing us to "participate in the divine nature" (2 Pet. 1:4). We practice it alongside other rituals of the church, but it is the central symbolic act in many worship services. It is anamnesis, it is a meal, and it consists of the most common elements of a first-century table: bread and wine. When it is not grape juice, the wine is usually port, and my friend loves to offer a carefully chosen one from Cyprus. The symbols are reminders of the physical body of Christ and the metaphorical body of Christ, the church. Tomes have been written on the subject, and my few words here do not suffice to describe its mystery.

The first time I celebrated the Lord's Supper, I was an over-confident intern at a church on Sanibel Island. I was scheduled to celebrate it in the early service and was a little annoyed that my mentor wanted me to practice it with him beforehand. I thought I knew Paul's words and would do an extemporaneous Eucharist seamlessly. I was wrong. This made me realize the careful attention I need to give to this ritual. Today I celebrate mostly extemporaneously, though we do share the words of the *Sursum Corda* (an opening exchange beginning with "Lift up your hearts") and the *Sanctus* (a proclamation of praise beginning with "Holy, holy, holy"). Every time, I am very careful to invest time into thinking about and practicing the celebration beforehand. It requires that I prepare not only the elements but also myself. Further, it invites the people to examine whether they are unified with others in the church. True, some receive the Eucharist with little thought or investment. But for those who do prepare and invest, the transformation is apparent.

And we pay attention. In many liturgies the Lord's Supper is the high point, the climax, of the worship; all that is done beforehand is simply leading to the Eucharist. We pay attention to Christ's institution of the Supper, how Christ's work transforms us. We receive and we give thanks.

The Eucharist is a deeply meaningful ritual with carefully chosen symbols and the four hallmarks of powerful rituals.

At-Church Ritual: Completing the Year

New Year's Day comes eight days after we celebrate Christ's birth. It is the day he was circumcised and named, and many churches celebrate it with a worship service. Just as Jesus was marked by circumcision as Jewish, we can also choose to mark the end of one year and the beginning of the next. This ritual can take place on (or close to) New Year's Day or at the end of the school year. The ritual pays attention to events that took place and accomplishments people made in the outgoing year. Each individual invests in the ritual by preparing a narrative about the year and obtaining an appropriate symbol to represent the year, and all participants also invest in listening to each other. The purpose is to be transformed from someone holding on to the outgoing year to someone who is ready for what is to come. A plant used in the ritual clearly symbolizes the life expected in the incoming year. This ritual can be repeated each year. The key progression is story, contemplation, release, and gratitude.

Completing the Year

Preparation

In order to sum up the year and move into the next, participants prepare a narrative that will consist of the following:

- What they gave life to in the outgoing year (accomplishments)
- How they received life this past year (great events, promotions, etc.)
- What was hard during the outgoing year (losses, difficult events)

Participants also purchase a plant with a pot that can be written on, and permanent markers should be available. Pots should be boldly labeled with the year (e.g., 2023, or 2022–2023 if it is a school year).

The Ritual

Leader: We gather together today to celebrate and process our previous year so we can freely move to the next. *Leader offers an extemporaneous prayer of invitation to the Holy Spirit.*

Each participant takes a turn sharing from their list, telling the narrative and writing key words with the permanent marker on the plant pot. All others listen without interruption.

Leader: I invite you to take a few moments of silence and observe your plant pot. Contemplate it and this past year in the presence of God. *Silence is kept for as long as deemed appropriate.*

All: Lord, grant me the ability to release what you desire I release from last year so that I may be ready to give and receive in this coming year. *Silence is kept.* Lord, grant me the serenity to accept the things I cannot change, the courage to change the things I can, and the wisdom to know the difference. Amen.[28]

Leader: *Extemporaneous prayer of gratitude for the past year and blessing on the year to come. Finish with this blessing:* I invite you to put out your hands in a gesture of receiving as I bless you. *Leader raises both hands in blessing:* "May the God of hope fill you with all joy and peace as you trust in him, so that you may overflow with hope by the power of the Holy Spirit" (Rom. 15:13).

Reflection on Rituals' Transformational Power

The following is intended as guided reflection for the evaluation and change of ritual practices, one ritual at a time (for individuals or small groups).

1. Begin with prayer, asking for God's wisdom in this exercise.
2. Reflect on the ritual using the following questions:
   - How do we conceptualize God's work and the human work in it?

- Does it rely only on words? If so, what gestures or symbols might enhance it?
- Does it fantasize, mythologize, or borrow wholesale?
- On a scale of one to ten, rate the ritual according to how it involves the community, number one meaning it is only individual and number ten meaning it involves the entire church community or target community.
- List and evaluate the investments that participants in the ritual make. Do you judge them sufficient? If not, brainstorm ideas on increasing the investment.
- List and evaluate the investments that the community makes in the ritual. Do you judge them sufficient? If not, brainstorm ideas on increasing the investment.
- List the symbols in the ritual and evaluate them. Are they carefully chosen, appropriate, and powerful? If not, brainstorm symbols that might be better.
- Rate, on a scale of one to ten, how well the ritual pays attention to what it recognizes or achieves. Does this need to be increased? If so, brainstorm how to do so.
- Ritual transformation is best evaluated with data. The most in-depth evaluation would incorporate qualitative or quantitative data from participants immediately after the rite and then a certain number of years later. We can gather this data if we deem it appropriate. Otherwise, transformation can be evaluated according to the intent of those who celebrate/ plan the ritual and the narrated experience of participants in the following manner:
    i. Clarify what transformation is desired. It may involve multiple planes.

122

2

    ii. Evaluate how the celebrants/planners sought to move toward this goal.

    iii. Evaluate it from the perspective of the participants (this information can be gathered by exit survey or informal conversation).

3. Create an action plan for ritual change.
4. End in prayer.

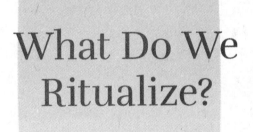

What Do We Ritualize?

6

Ends

I HAVE ALWAYS BEEN IN EDUCATION: first as a student, then as a teacher, and now as a professor. The rhythm of the school year is my life pattern. September is the beginning, winter is the middle, and June is the end. June is also the beginning of an unstructured summer that ends around August 31.

Sometimes I love this yearly structure. At the end of every semester, I get to look back and observe successes and failures. And then I get to begin again with the intention of maximizing successes and minimizing failures. What other profession offers such frequent time for reevaluation?

Sometimes I hate it. There is so much change, and even good change is stressful. In 1967, T. H. Holmes and R. H. Rahe developed a scale that rates the effect of specific life changes on people's stress level. They rated forty-three events from greater stress to less stress.[1] Marriage is ranked number seven, pregnancy is twelve, and an outstanding personal achievement is twenty-five. These are generally considered good changes, but they still cause stress, and a combination of stressors can lead to physical illness.[2] Change is stressful.

August usually finds me grumpy. I find time in the summer to write, work, and have fun, all on my own schedule. The prospect of September's confined schedule and work done in an office rather than my beautiful backyard gets me down. My ritual helps.

I am writing this in August, and in a few weeks, my kids and I will sit down with some construction paper and markers to make our book entitled "The Abdallah Family Summer 2022." In it we will write and illustrate all we enjoyed this summer. Then we will read it together and put it on the shelf with the past years' books. Ritually marking the end of summer transforms my grumpiness into satisfaction and prepares me to begin the new year.

We are beginning part 3, which contains three chapters that focus on what to ritualize, building on the foundations of why and how we ritualize. We will explore transitions: ends, middles, and beginnings, because they pepper all of life, are challenging, and are opportunities for transformation. I will provide a separate chapter for each of these categories as if they happen in a neat order, even though our lives tend not to be neat and orderly. Some beginnings happen before ends, as when we begin a new job while still training the new person at our old job; some middles feel interminable as we suffer long-term unemployment or chronic illness; sometimes there seems to be no middle at all.

Ends are beginnings, and beginnings are ends; the appropriate title for the ritual that ends years of study is called "commencement." Middles for those with chronic or terminal illness may also be beginnings and ends. I will include a Jesuit priest's idea of a ritual for marking the beginning of palliative care in the "Beginnings" chapter and will also include a ritual for marking a liminal state such as chronic illness in the "Middles" chapter.

Retirement is usually considered to be an event that ends an era of working and opens a new era. Psychologist and transitions guru Nancy Schlossberg, however, sees it as a three-stage process: an end, a middle, and a beginning. The actual retirement is the end, the "moving out" or letting go of a work role, and is followed by "moving through," which is an adjustment to the new phase, which she found took at least two years. Finally, there is "moving in," or creating a new life of meaning in retirement.[3] Even though retirement is often considered one event, it is experienced as a process that takes years. Schlossberg recommends we observe how much a transition affects our roles, relationships, routines, and assumptions, and she says we can figure out how much attention to pay to adjusting.[4] This advice is helpful: the more a transition affects our roles, relationships, routines, and assumptions, the more we need ritual to help us through.

Ends, middles, and beginnings are inextricably intertwined, deeply interrelated, and often unpredictable and messy. They share several characteristics, and ritual helps us embrace our journey of transitions.

The Bible and Transitions

Thus far this book has sought to interweave the biblical story, theology, psychology, ritual theory, and personal experience. My overall suggestion to create transformative rituals to pastor people through transition is a response to felt need, not a biblical imperative. It is possible that life transitions were ritualized by the Israelites or early Christians and that the rituals were living and not written because traditional societies' rituals are engraved in the bones of the people. For example, one of the many questions we have about the story of Jephthah's daughter in Judges 11 pertains to what the ritual of roaming the hills and weeping with her friends entailed. There was no need to explain or interpret this ritual, as it was presumably known to readers. As such, I cannot point to one overall paradigm from the Bible to show how we should ritualize ends, middles, and beginnings. Life-cycle rituals are seldom described, and we receive only small snapshots from the lives of most people in the Bible.

If I wanted to stretch the stories to fit the paradigm, I could say that the time Jesus spent in the temple when he was around twelve was an end to childhood, there were silent years of preparation in the middle, and the beginning of his ministry was his baptism. I could say, further, that his death and resurrection marked the end of his earthly ministry; he appeared to many over forty days in the middle, before his ascension; and the Holy Spirit's descent at day fifty (Pentecost) is often understood as the beginning of the church. Likewise, Moses's time in Egypt ended when he killed the Egyptian, his forty years of preparation in the desert was the middle, and then the burning bush began his ministry. At times, ends, middles, and beginnings are somewhat clear in the Bible but are not necessarily ritualized.

Part 3, then, will tend to draw from several snapshots of human stories in the Bible that portray people experiencing an end, middle, or beginning. They will primarily be illustrative of the transitional concepts described and may not include a ritual.

Change versus Transition

I jokingly told the publisher of my first book that my next would be called *Transitions Suck!* I suppose a book about rituals that transform sounds a lot better than *Transitions Suck!* Still, this book is based on the idea that transitions and other life events are challenging and that rituals help.

William Bridges is an authority on change and transition. He makes a distinction between the two that is helpful for our purposes: "Change is situational: the move to a new site, a new CEO replaces the founder. . . . Transition, on the other hand, is psychological; it is a three-phase process that people go through as they internalize and come to terms with the details of the new situation that the change brings about."[5] There it is again: a three-stage process.

Our exploration of rites of passage called these three stages separation, transition, and reincorporation. Our lives are full of ends, murky middles, and beginnings. Ritualizing them helps us bring clarity and purpose as we seek to recognize our embodiment along our individual journey of life. My exposition of *Woman* focused on the beginning. Here I begin with ends.

Beginning with ends is an idea I borrow from Bridges. His second rule of transitions is "Every transition begins with an ending," and his fourth is "First there is an ending, *then* a beginning, and an important empty or fallow time in between." Bridges even finds these transitions in the order of nature (fall, winter, spring).[6] This idea is echoed in the words of Scripture where death precedes rebirth or resurrection. In the Gospel of John, Jesus states, "Very truly I tell you, unless a kernel of wheat falls to the ground and dies, it remains only a single seed. But if it dies, it produces many seeds" (John 12:24). Jesus's death and resurrection is the central tenet of the Christian faith, Paul declares himself crucified but still alive (Gal. 2:20), and our death to sin and rebirth to new life is pictured in the ritual of baptism. Christians are very familiar with death and rebirth, with ends followed by beginnings.

Ends are first. Every beginning is preceded by an end, just as the beginning of my school year follows the end of summer. Ends involve grief and loss, though Western culture prefers to ignore the negative emotions and celebrate only the beginning.

Believer baptism signifies both an end and a beginning: the end of our old way of life and the beginning of the new. While we may acknowledge the change from the old, we seldom acknowledge that it may involve grief and loss, like the loss of familial connections due to following Christ.

We celebrate physical birth, but the baby cries, thrust out of a safe and warm environment to breathe air and work for food. We celebrate parenthood and expect new moms and dads to be happy with this beginning, but we do not always recognize the end. In Bridges's first seminar on transitions, a new mom declared, "I really do love the baby, but the old freedom and easiness are gone. We can't take off any longer whenever we please, or even live by our own schedules. . . . It seems to me that I've crossed some kind of threshold and there's no going back. My old life has gone. How come nobody talks about that? They congratulate you on your new life, but I have to mourn the old life alone."[7] New parenthood involves an unrecognized end that professor and grief expert Kenneth Doka calls disenfranchised grief.

Disenfranchised Ends

Every culture has rules or norms that govern which ends are legitimately grieved. Human death is generally legitimate, or "enfranchised," grief.[8] The surrounding culture enfranchises it through employers' paid leave, airlines' bereavement fares, family and friends' attention and presence, and the church's ritual and support. "The rite of a funeral publicly testifies and affirms the right to grieve."[9] Even in death, however, there are rules that create degrees of legitimate grief. Employers' leave pertains only to people who have specific relationships with the deceased. We internalize these cultural norms and judge our subjective grief over deaths with statements like, "I have a right to be sad," or, "Why am I so sad about this?"[10]

When we have a grief response that we do not feel is allowed, we are likely experiencing "disenfranchised" grief, defined as "grief that results when a person experiences a significant loss and the resultant grief is not openly acknowledged, socially validated, or publicly mourned. In short, although the individual is experiencing a grief reaction, there is no social recognition that the person has a right to grieve or a claim for social sympathy or support."[11] With regard to death, the grief of an ex-spouse or an engaged partner is disenfranchised.[12]

Employers do not give leave, there is no lower airfare, and there is no ritual for broken engagements, miscarriages and stillbirths, the death of pets, job loss, divorce, an empty nest, and many other losses we experience across our lifespan. "The problem of disenfranchised grief can be expressed in a paradox: The nature of disenfranchised grief creates additional problems for grief, while removing or minimizing sources of support."[13] This chapter is about ends and pays particular attention to disenfranchised ones. How can Christian rituals help people at these times?

Characteristics of Ends

I attended a wedding this past weekend, briefly greeting those I knew in the narthex and quickly entering the church. Leaving the reception, however, took much longer. We wanted to bid farewell to the bride and groom but had to wait because they were in the middle of a special dance. While we waited, we said goodbye to new acquaintances and we embraced old friends, telling them how delightful it had been to see them and reiterating invitations to spend more time together. Whenever I am in a social situation, it takes more time to say goodbye than to say hello. Ritualizing ends is about saying goodbye well, and it takes time. Ends are not easy, as they are characterized by actual and metaphorical death as well as grief and continuing bonds.

Actual and Metaphorical Death

We are accustomed to ritualizing physical death. At the death of Aaron, Moses ritually instates Aaron's son Eleazar to the priesthood, and then all mourn Aaron for thirty days (Num. 20:22–29). Job's friends do a form of "sitting *shiva*" with him in silence for seven days, a tradition still practiced in Judaism when someone dies (Job 2:11–13). The women are at Jesus's tomb at dawn to perform the common care for his body at death (Luke 24:1–3). Our funerals ritualize actual death, but some ends involve metaphorical death, not physical death.

Three months into my first engagement, I called it off. I knew it was the right thing to do, but it felt absolutely awful. It meant death to a key life relationship and to the hopes and dreams that surrounded our plans. I was awash with complex emotions of loss, shame, hopelessness, and even despair. I usually wept alone, but my friends offered compassion, kindness, and, yes, a ritual.

Four months later, on the date of the hoped-for wedding, I had what we called a ritual burning. It was March in New York and a great night to be cozy by the fire. I had written a grief journal that explained all I had lost, and I had brought items I wanted to burn to symbolize the death of the relationship and my choice to let go. I read the journal to my friends, burned the items, and prayed, and then we relaxed by the fire with some wine and cheese. It was really difficult and really, really freeing.

Traditional rites of passage involve symbolic death and a separation from that which once was. Adolescent rites of passage help the individual bid farewell to childhood and welcome adulthood. But saying goodbye to childhood is not the only developmental loss we experience. Judith McCoyd, Jeanne Koller, and Carolyn Walter catalog non-death (usually disenfranchised) losses for each developmental stage. "Loss is at the heart of life and growth," they assert, and "normal maturational changes are recognized not only as growth, but also as a special form of loss in which one is expected to delight in the growth and ignore the loss aspect of the change, a perspective we challenge. The customary, destabilizing force of loss promotes self-reflection and this can lead to growth, particularly when the mourner's experience is validated and supported."[14] They desire to recognize these losses without requiring overt mourning.[15]

In addition to normal maturational losses, McCoyd, Koller, and Walter mention losses such as unemployment, changes in identity, parental divorce or personal divorce, and moving to another home. These are all metaphorical deaths, and while we might follow their advice about overt mourning not being *required*, why not offer the possibility of ritual to symbolize the death, leaving, or letting go? These losses are subjectively experienced, so some may have an easier time moving through them by engaging in overt mourning rituals conducted in community.

Bridges states that metaphorical death involves "disengagement, dismantling, disidentification, disenchantment, and disorientation,"[16] none of which sound fun. Disengagement means separating oneself from the past, dismantling and disidentification involve letting go of identity markers from the past, disenchantment means realizing the past was not everything one thought it was, and disorientation involves letting go of previous ways of knowing where and who one is.[17] This is the end; this is the taking leave. When we neither recognize nor ritualize this, we do not end well. We, as Christians, should recognize and ritualize this symbolic death not because it is fun but because we believe in death and rebirth; we believe that the death of our Lord Jesus Christ preceded his resurrection and that we will follow him; we believe baptism is death to the old and life in the new. Metaphorical death is central to Christian life, and like the new mother in Bridges's seminar, we cannot go back.

135

Anxiety, Grief, and Sadness

Mark Searle sees the journey of conversion as leaving a safe shore and launching out into the deep; it involves an end.[18] "Unless we are seized, as when we fall in love, with a powerful hope that that which lies ahead will outweigh the sacrifice of what we are leaving behind, the inevitable result is panic. We panic because of what we are losing and are filled with anxiety in the face of the unknown that lies ahead."[19] There is the possibility of anxiety in ends, middles, and beginnings; it is helpful to know that rituals help alleviate anxiety, as we learned in chapter 3.

Not only is there anxiety, but there is grief and sadness in the face of an end. Grief is uncomfortable and "involves psychic pain, challenges in coping, and irritation, sadness, and rumination," as well as a sense of vulnerability and fear.[20] Psychology offers several models of grief; the most widely known is Elisabeth Kübler-Ross's five stages of denial, anger, bargaining, depression, and acceptance. She is often misinterpreted, since she developed this model for those losing their own lives, not for those who had lost loved ones.[21] More helpful than her five-stages model for our purposes is the dual-process model: grief involves going back and forth between loss orientation (LO) and restoration orientation (RO).[22] When the grief is fresh or is refreshed by some circumstance, LO is more frequent. RO strengthens as time passes, but LO still exists. Ritual can help us recognize and process both orientations in one event.

Choosing when and how to do a ritual may depend on the strength of LO and RO. This spring I had a loss that devastated me. It was the loss of something for which I had worked very hard, and I had hoped for the life transformation it would bring. It was also something of a sensitive nature, and the details were known only to a select few. When the loss happened, I plunged into LO. I read Psalm 13 every day: "How long, Lord? Will you forget me forever? How long will you hide your face from me? How long must I wrestle with my thoughts and day after day have sorrow in my heart?" (vv. 1–2). I knew I had to let go ritually, but I was not ready. Finally, I headed to the Hudson River with a pot of flower petals. Growing roses takes a lot of work, and we have many in our garden. To encourage new growth, we frequently deadhead the old flowers; these discarded petals were the ones I brought to the river. They symbolized the work I had done, the loss, and the hope of new growth. The Hudson, a mile away from my house, is three miles wide, is brackish, and has a four-foot tide, which means that it flows back and forth. My kids and I threw the petals into the water, saying goodbye to that which I had lost. They floated down, but who knows? Perhaps they also floated back with the tide and the opportunity might renew itself. It helped me make meaning of the loss and trust God.

Bridges asserts, "Endings must be dealt with if we are to move on to whatever comes next in our lives. . . . No longer ritualized and formally prepared for us, endings happen to us in unforeseeable ways that often seem devoid of meaning—much less a positive meaning."[23] Psychologist Pauline Boss recommends six action guidelines for finding resilience in the face of loss, one of which is finding meaning.[24] Ritual is a way of finding meaning, as is storytelling,[25] which we will explore in the next chapter, on middles.

Rather than ignoring the anxiety, grief, and sadness of ends, we can respond to difficult emotions and make meaning through ritual. Psychologist Susan David points out that emotions are useful and recommends paying attention. If we are falsely cheerful and suppress sadness, for example, we deny ourselves the guidance that sadness gives and possibly the help from others who perceive our grief.[26]

As a child I learned the shortest verse in the Bible: "Jesus wept" (John 11:35). In John 11 Jesus's good friend Lazarus dies,

Jesus is confronted by Lazarus's sisters Mary and Martha for not being there to heal him, and then he comes to the tomb and weeps. The word translated "weep" is used only once in the Greek New Testament and refers to the shedding of tears. Jesus is confronted with a huge loss and is moved by his friends' grief, and there he is, outside the tomb, tears falling down his face. We have many images of the serious Jesus and some of the joyful Jesus, but I have never seen one of the tearful Jesus. But the tearful Jesus teaches us.

I often wonder why Jesus weeps outside the grave when in a few moments he will raise Lazarus from the dead. Perhaps he weeps because Lazarus will die again and human sin makes this world a place of sadness and weeping. Perhaps he weeps because of his love for all the world and especially Martha, Mary, and Lazarus. Jesus clearly shares his friends' grief. In the same way that we assume Jesus laughed even though the Gospels never record him laughing, I think that Jesus wept a lot more often than in this one event and that we can learn from him when we face ends.

Continuing Bonds

Ends are paradoxical because they do not signal a full stop. Life offers no full closure. In the simple example of the end of summer, the memories still exist and will warm me on winter days when we reread the summer scrapbook. In the case of death, acknowledging continuing bonds with the deceased helps us move forward.[27] Our bonds are not the same as they were in life, but they still exist, even beyond death. Boss recommends that we revise the attachment to our loved one, not sever it.[28] We can say goodbye to the physical closeness and embodied companionship a loved one offered. We do not, however, close the door on memories or the impact this person had and continues to have on our lives. The founder of attachment theory, John

138

Bowlby, pointed out the poignant paradox: when a widow or widower allows their feelings for their dead spouse to continue, it helps them meaningfully reorganize their lives. Maintaining previous bonds helps us continue our lives well, even into new relationships.[29]

The first wedding I was honored to officiate was between two of my close friends. Leading up to the wedding, it became clear that the husband-to-be needed a ritual to facilitate an end before this new beginning. I wanted to ensure that he had let go of his previous wife and felt reconciled to God. He had been married in the church with friends and family and then divorced in a courtroom, alone.[30] I wanted to corporately declare his reconciliation with God and the church and to revise his relationship with his ex-wife by marking the end through ritual.

He and his first wife had two wonderful kids, and he wanted to make sure that letting go of her in the divorce ritual did not entail letting go of them. I assured him that he did not lose them or the great memories he had of his previous marriage. The ritual allowed him to reconcile himself to God and revise his relationship with his ex-wife through recognizing the divorce. There is no complete closure in this type of loss, but there is a revision of bonds and a negotiation of their continuance. The at-church ritual below is an adaptation of how we marked this end together.

Sometimes we prefer that the bonds not continue. In the case of my broken-off engagement, I hoped that I could forget the relationship with the man who had been my fiancé. About two years after the breakup, he died. Neither of us had yet moved on to new relationships, and I was invited to be closely involved in the grieving process with his family and friends; my college community supported this involvement in multiple ways. It was another revision of our attachment. Today I am happily married with kids, so the continuing bonds are weak. They served their purpose to help me move on.

Embracing Ends

So, how do we embrace the ends that pepper our lives? I have already hinted at the first step: embrace sadness. I did this best with the help of a therapist because I had pushed away sadness for most of my life. Research shows that embracing sadness actually brings greater happiness. "If we aim to avoid sadness, even a little, we limit our existence and put ourselves at greater risk of normal sadness tipping over into something more serious."[31] In fact, fighting sadness makes the sadness worse.[32] Helen Russell's *How to Be Sad* engages multiple practical hints for being sad better.

Ritual helps us embrace the sadness that ends inevitably bring. Funerals have many functions, including the acknowledgment of the reality of the loss and the provision of opportunities to say goodbye and to express sadness, gratitude, and anger, all in community.[33] They offer a patterned ritual that supports us as we express our sadness and other complex emotions.[34] They help us find meaning in our grief and symbolically connect us with our loved one.[35]

Grief over human death is usually enfranchised by the funeral, but not always. In the case of miscarriage and stillbirth, we lack rituals, and this lack "has consequences as the mother and her supporters try (mostly in vain) to either move on without acknowledgement (difficult because the mother [and father are] feeling loss) or find new ways of observing the loss."[36] Human ritualizers often invent their own ritual to observe the loss.

The church, however, can serve parents during both miscarriage and stillbirth. Puneet Singh, Kearsley Stewart, and Scott Moses declare that rituals do help parents say goodbye: "One of the psychological functions of funerals for stillborn children is to help parents achieve 'reality confrontation,' or accept their child as real so that they can then grieve for the loss and integrate it into their lives."[37] They gathered data from ministers about how they ritualized miscarriage and stillbirth. Some had no ritual response, some adapted the funeral ritual, some created new rituals, and some included a rite of baptism for the baby. The ritual I include below adapts portions of funeral rituals and prayers and has some original portions as well.

The grief I experienced over the rupture of my engagement and my fiancé's subsequent death would normally be disenfranchised. I would be encouraged to move on to the "other fish in the sea" and would certainly not have an honored place at his funeral. Admittedly, some parts of the funeral and planning process were a little awkward. However, Doka argues that even when the larger culture disenfranchises a certain kind of loss, smaller subcultures might actually enfranchise it and allow for the expression of grief.[38] My subculture enfranchised my grief, first through a small group of friends and then through the larger college community, both by means of ritual. This was transformative for me, and I dream of a community that honors both enfranchised and disenfranchised loss well.

At-Church Ritual: Miscarriage or Stillbirth

This ritual will help enfranchise the grief that accompanies miscarriage and stillbirth as a loss recognized by ritual and communal mourning. The service itself is formal but adaptable. The key progression includes declaration of God as our hope, acknowledgment and recounting of the child's life, prayer for the child, parental declarations and lament, prayer of healing for the parents, communion, and blessing. Parents may create a symbolic memorial; a possibility is described below.

Miscarriage or Stillbirth

Preparation

Parents are invited to do the following:

- Name the child.
- Prepare the story of the child's life, including prayers, hopes, and fears that preceded his or her conception and all that followed until the time of his/her death.
- Consider using a symbolic memorial such at this: The parents write a letter to the child that rejoices in his or her life and also print a photo (or ultrasound) of the child and/or parents. The letter and photos will be placed in a scrapbook or a frame of the parents' choosing. They can be displayed at the service and kept in a special place by the parents in their home.
- Parents should familiarize themselves with, and prepare themselves for, their parts in the service.
- Parents invite family, close friends, and a spiritual leader who will guide the ritual.

Scripture Reading and Invocation

Leader: On behalf of (child's) parents, (names), I welcome you here today to honor the life of (child), cut short at only (age). Please stand in body or spirit as we read the Scripture together:[39]

All:

I am the resurrection and the life, says the Lord;

The one that believes in me, though s/he were dead, yet shall s/he live;

and whoever lives and believes in me shall never die.

I know that my Redeemer lives,

and that the Lord shall stand at the latter day upon the earth;

and though this body be destroyed, yet shall I see God.

Leader: Let us pray. (*Leader prays an invocation that invites God's presence and blessing on this time.*) Sin and death entered

142

the world hand in hand. You and I have never known life without sin and death. There are times that we can live well alongside this reality, and there are other times when we feel the sting of sin and death acutely. This is one of the latter times. When a person who has lived a long, full life passes on, we miss the person, and we are thankful for their life. But when a person's life is snuffed out before it really begins, we rage, we weep, we search for answers. Why? We miss this person's presence, but that is not all. We miss what could have been and never had a chance to be. When a budding life is lost in the womb, this missing can be unbearable. Some call the grief illegitimate, but for many it's crippling. A mother may feel betrayed by her body; a mother and father may feel betrayed by God. Fear and grief return at the advent of any new pregnancy, and the life lost turns parents' lives upside down. We gather today to witness that grief, to mourn the loss of life, and to turn to our only hope in life and in death, Jesus Christ our Redeemer.

Parents: *(Tell the story of the child's life.)*

Leader: We believe that God is rich in mercy, full of compassion, and abounding in grace. So, joining with David, who mourned the loss of his son, we acknowledge that we cannot bring this child back. We also declare with David that though she/he will not come to us, we will go to her/him. We believe that she/he has died in the Lord and is alive. Jesus said to the thief on the cross, "Today you will be with me in paradise" (Luke 23:43). We believe she/he is with Jesus today. (Parents' names), your child is in the arms of our good God, whose only begotten and coeternal Son became human unto death and has given us hope of resurrection and life eternal. And so we pray for her/him,

> O God, whose beloved Son took little children into his arms and blessed them: Give us grace to entrust this child (name) to your never-failing care and love and bring us all to your heavenly kingdom. Remember the soul of your departed child. Baptize him/her in the sea of your generosity and save him/her by your ineffable grace. We ask this through the same Son Jesus Christ our Lord, who lives and reigns with you and the Holy Spirit, one God, now and forever. Amen.[40]

Leader: In light of your loss, what are you asking God about?
Parents: (*Respond.*)
Leader: In light of your loss, what are you anxious about?
Parents: (*Respond.*)
Leader: Songs of lament make up about two-thirds of the book of Psalms. They declare that all is not right with the world and ask God to fix it. They then declare their trust in God and end in hope. We all know that grief can be cyclical; one day we're able to hope, while the next day we're not. But to declare that these parents' journey is one toward hope in God, they will read this lament psalm together.
Parents: (*Read Psalm 13 together.*)
Leader: In light of your loss, what are you lamenting?
Parents: (*Respond.*)
Leader: Let us pray for (parents' names), parents of (child's name). Almighty and gracious God, who gave up your only begotten Son to death, comfort these, your children, as they grieve their loss. Remind them that Christ took up our pain and bore our suffering that we might be healed (Isa. 53:4–5). Walk with them in this time of grief, and comfort as only you can comfort. We pray that as you find community in yourself, Father, Son, Holy Spirit, this family would find deep community with one another and among the faithful. Jesus, you were born of the Virgin Mary, and as an infant you were laid in a manger. In your great mercy, have regard for your servant (mother's name), who has miscarried that which was conceived in her. Heal her suffering and grant to her, O loving Lord, health and strength of body and soul. Send your angels to guard her from every assault of sickness and weakness and all inward torment. You who accept the innocence of infancy in your kingdom, comfort the minds of these your servants and grant them peace.[41] Amen.

Communion

Leader: It is fitting that the journey of this service concludes in communion. At this table we declare these truths: Death yields life. Suffering brings hope. This world is not all there is. Let us also declare for ourselves and for (child's name) the New City Catechism[42] answer to the question, "What is our only hope in life and in death?"

All: That we are not our own but belong, body and soul, both in life and death, to God our Savior Jesus Christ.

Communion is prepared and people served according to the tradition of the church. If the tradition allows, the parents of the child serve the communicants.

Prayer of Thanksgiving

All: Almighty God, we thank you that in your great love you have fed us with the spiritual food and drink of the body and blood of your Son Jesus Christ, and have given us a foretaste of your heavenly banquet. Grant that this sacrament may be to us a comfort in affliction and a pledge of our inheritance in that kingdom where there is no death, neither sorrow nor crying, but the fullness of joy with all your saints; through Jesus Christ our Savior. Amen.[43]

Leader closes with an extemporaneous benediction.

With-Friends Ritual: Divorce

Christians get married in the church—or, if elsewhere, at least by a minister—and divorced in a courtroom by a judge. This ritual is intended to acknowledge the end of the marriage by the church and provide both reconciliation and a forward path for the divorcee. It starts with reconciliation with God, not because the divorcee is necessarily unreconciled but in order to meet a felt need for the declaration of reconciliation. The key progression is reconciliation, release, healing, freedom, and communion.

Divorce

Preparation

Both divorcee and witnesses shall be familiar with their parts in the rite. The divorcee may want to symbolically surrender any symbols (e.g., a ring) that declared his or her unity with the previous spouse.

Invocation

After a brief explanation of the purpose of the ritual and its progression, the leader prays a prayer of invocation.

Rite of Reconciliation[44]

All: Have mercy on us, O God, according to your loving-kindness;
    in your great compassion blot out our offenses.
Wash us through and through from our wickedness,
    and cleanse us from our sin.
For we know our transgressions only too well,
    and our sin is ever before us.

Leader: Hear the Word of God to all who truly turn to [God]: "Come to me, all ye that travail and are heavy laden, and I will refresh you" (Matt. 11:28).

All: Holy God, you formed us from the dust in your image and likeness and redeemed us from sin and death by the cross of your Son Jesus Christ. Through the water of baptism you clothed us with the shining garment of his righteousness and established us among your children in your kingdom. Most merciful God, we confess that we have sinned against you in thought, word, and deed, by what we have done and by what we have left undone. We have not loved you with our whole heart; we have not loved our neighbors as ourselves.

Divorcee: Especially, I confess to you and to the church . . . (*Here the divorcee confesses particular sins with regard to his or her former marriage in silence or out loud. The witnesses confess silently.*)

All: Therefore, O Lord, from these and all other sins I cannot now remember, I turn to you in sorrow and repentance. Receive me again into the arms of your mercy and restore me to the blessed company of your faithful people; through him in whom you have redeemed the world, your Son our Savior Jesus Christ. Amen.

All pray the Lord's Prayer.

Forgiveness and Release

Leader: The Greek word in the Lord's Prayer that is translated "forgive" means "to let go" or "to send away" or "to keep no longer." Do you, then, forgive (former spouse), who also sinned against you?

Divorcee: I forgive (former spouse); I let her/him go; I keep her/him no longer.

Leader: (*Laying hands on divorcee*) "If [you] confess [your] sins, [God] is faithful and just and will forgive [you your] sins and purify [you] from all unrighteousness" (1 John 1:9). Our Lord Jesus Christ absolves you and restores you in the perfect peace of the church. Amen.

Each witness, individually: (*Making eye contact with divorcee*) (Divorcee's name), you are forgiven, released from your previous marriage vows, and reconciled to God.

Rite of Healing

Leader: (*Making eye contact with divorcee*) (Divorcee), there were great parts to your (number)-year marriage with (former spouse), the greatest being (children). Though you are letting go of (former spouse), you are not losing the good that came from having a family and that continues in your children.[45] As you forgive and let go, some wounds will need to be healed. (*Leader takes anointing oil and explains its use in healing prayers as explained in James 5. Leader then anoints the divorcee on the forehead, making the shape of a cross and saying the following.*) (Divorcee), "I lay my hands upon you in the name of the Father and of the Son and of the Holy Spirit, asking our Lord Jesus Christ to sustain you with his presence, to drive away all sickness of body and spirit, and to give you that victory of life and peace that will enable you to serve him both now and evermore. Amen."[46]

Declarations of Freedom

The following declarations are intended to declare truth in contrast to lies the divorcee may believe; they are representative examples and may be changed as needed.

Leader: (Divorcee), you made vows long ago, and they have been broken in ways you could not control. We mourn that, but we confess the truth.

Witnesses: You are a (man/woman) of your word.

Divorcee: I am a (man/woman) of my word.

Leader: (Divorcee), you have been separated from your children, whom you love deeply, in ways you could not control. We mourn that and will continue to mourn with you, but we also confess the truth.

Witnesses: You are an excellent father/mother.

Divorcee: I am an excellent father/mother.

Leader: (Divorcee), you are confused about the reasons for (former spouse) leaving. You wonder if you could have stopped it, and you are searching for some flaw in your actions, some flaw in your upbringing, some flaw hidden in the depths of you. We confess the truth.

Witnesses: You have no flaw that we don't have, and you have become more like Jesus since (former spouse) left.

Divorcee: I have no flaw that you don't have, and I have become more like Jesus since (former spouse) left.

Leader: (Divorcee), you feel like you deserve punishment for whatever you did to contribute to the divorce, but we confess the truth.

Witnesses: Christ took your punishment for you so that you could be free, and you are worthy to be loved and appreciated.

Divorcee: Christ took my punishment for me so that I could be free, and I am worthy to be loved and appreciated.

Leader: (Divorcee), you think that because (former spouse) divorced you, you are destined for another divorce. We confess the truth.

Witnesses: You are destined for lasting love and marriage.

Divorcee: I am destined for lasting love and marriage. (*Divorcee has an opportunity to renounce any continuing false beliefs.*)

Witnesses: (Divorcee), God has freed you from the lies. We urge you, then: live in freedom!

Rite of Communion

Communion is shared according to the tradition of those present.

Words of Blessing

All witnesses may offer words of blessing to divorcee. Leader finishes with a benediction.

7

Middles

WHEN I WAS TWENTY-SIX, I went to seminary because I wanted
to work with the church in Buenos Aires. I had lived in Asun-
ción, Paraguay, but I loved the way the people of Buenos Aires
sang Spanish, and I wanted to work with the evangelical movement there. My sending agency required seminary, so I went.

I graduated with a master of divinity in 2002. And as often
happens with education, what brought me there was not quite
what was taking me away. I was no longer sure of my calling
to overseas missionary work and had accepted a position to
teach Bible at Nyack College. One day I met with the director
of missionary candidates. I remember it well. We were in the
conference room, which had a view of the wide Hudson River,
and were sitting at the long table with stately blue leather chairs.
We chatted about my direction and my questions, and he did
not tell me what to do. He did not try to convince me that I was
great and that the sending agency wanted—no, needed—me.
He listened, reflected, and then advised that I learn to tolerate
ambiguity.

Did my anger show on my face? I'll never know, but this was not the counsel I desired. Like many Americans, I dislike ambiguity. I want closure; I want certainty; I want the decisions of my life to be wrapped up with a neat bow so I can easily walk my path. Little did I know that a tolerance for ambiguity is, in fact, a recipe for resilience.

Ambiguity is a characteristic of what social scientists call a liminal state, a place betwixt and between where we were and where we are going. I was no longer sure I wanted to work with the church in Buenos Aires; I had a new job teaching at a college, but I was not sure that was my goal either. I felt precarious, about to fall into an abyss of nothingness and confusion. Ambiguity and liminality can be like that when we have no tolerance for it.

Liminal states are times of waiting, and during them we often do not know when the outcome we desire will occur. In the book of Genesis, Abraham and Sarah wait for Isaac for twenty-five years. When Abraham is seventy-five years old, God promises him blessing and offspring and calls him to leave his people and land. When he arrives in Canaan, God appears again and promises offspring, and Abraham builds an altar and worships God. This ritual marks his action of faith and God's promise (Gen. 12:1–9). Later God appears again, and Abraham questions him because he and Sarah still have no child. God reiterates the promise of offspring and cuts the covenant with him (Gen. 15). After waiting eleven years after God's initial promise, Sarah still has no child, so she offers her servant Hagar to Abraham, and Hagar bears him Ishmael (Gen. 16). While this manner of producing children is common practice at the time, it is problematic in multiple ways. Sometimes we respond to the ambiguity, complex emotions, and vulnerability of the liminal state in ways that do not benefit us. When Ishmael is thirteen, Abraham ninety-nine, and Sarah ninety, God changes their names and requires male circumcision and obedience, and within the year Sarah gives birth to Isaac (Gen. 17:1–18:15; 21:1–6). God's renaming them and the symbolic act of circumcision ritually usher in the fulfillment of the promise after twenty-five years of liminality.

I introduced liminality in chapter 1 as the middle stage of a rite of passage and gave the examples of engagement (between singleness and marriage) and college (between high school and the "real world"). Van Gennep likens it to a threshold: standing in the doorway between one place and another, having already stepped out of the previous structured reality but not yet having stepped into the new structured reality.[1] Liminality is the "already but not yet" between the end and the beginning.

I write this while on the train to New York City. I thought I boarded the express, but I was using an old train schedule. I realized my error when I experienced all the local stops. I am still going to New York, but I will arrive later than anticipated. Liminality is like that—it often lasts longer than we think it will. The slowness of the train encouraged me to notice each stop, each step in the process toward the goal. The stops told me where I was and signaled progress. Rituals are like that. They give us opportunity to recognize where we are on this journey of life. They are particularly helpful when we are in a liminal state, confused about whether we are making any progress toward whatever might be next.

What Liminality Feels Like

I once heard Billy Graham state that Jesus was the only person born to die. Of course, the effects of the incarnation, life, death, and resurrection of Jesus Christ differ from the effects of our lives, but every person who is born will die. The time we spend in the liminal space between birth and death varies, and we are often able to embrace or even ignore our lifetime of liminal ambiguity.

Within each earthly life other periods of liminality also exist, like engagement, education, pregnancy, relocation, job transition, and more. Some even experience liminality in the more minute basics of life, like the commute home or the pause that occurs when one party conversation ends and we move to chat with others.

Communitas

Ritual theorist Victor Turner seems to love liminality. Without it, ritual transformation is impossible. It is in the liminal space that creativity is cultivated and the new is birthed; it is the place of innovation for ritual and culture. For Turner, liminality is a value and maybe even a virtue.[2]

Turner's work is groundbreaking in its attention to *communitas*, the special nonhierarchical community created when individuals share a liminal state. Even though *communitas* is often temporary, it can also be more enduring, like the group of college friends who stick together for life. Christian monks and nuns, however, choose perpetual liminality and form *communitas* that is a permanent family. When St. Francis began the First Order of mendicant monks, he called the group to live in a perpetual state of liminal poverty and wandering, like Christ.[3] For Turner, this was the optimal place of *communitas*, a structureless existence. While the survival of the order required some sort of structure,[4] the value of continued liminality in community is visible in monastic orders. Turner's liminality is creative and relational.

This creative and relational community is clear in Jesus's ministry with his disciples. Between "Follow me" and "It is finished," they wandered with no home, received support and sustenance from others, and were transformed.[5] They bonded deeply with one another.

Opposites Mixed Together

Unlike Turner, I rather dislike liminality. Sure, the liminality of engagement might have exciting parties and showers, but real bridezillas preexisted the reality show because confusion and anxiety may be just as common as joy during engagement. Sure, college friends may be the closest friends we ever have in our lives, but fear of failure and sleepless nights are also characteristic of the liminal educational state. I especially dislike liminality when I do not experience it with a community or when I do not know what is next. "How long, LORD?" (Ps. 13:1) is a common cry of the psalmist that we can apply to unchosen or undesired liminal states. Like liminality, lament psalms contain opposites, such as disillusionment and optimism.[6]

In 1 Samuel 1, the Lord has closed Hannah's womb. Hannah is deeply loved by her husband Elkanah but ridiculed for her infertility by Elkanah's other, fertile wife, Peninnah. Year after year, when Elkanah takes his whole family to worship at Shiloh, where the tabernacle is, the bully Peninnah provokes Hannah until she weeps and cannot eat. Elkanah's comment "Don't I mean more to you than ten sons?" (1 Sam. 1:8) does not comfort her. She weeps bitterly in her deep anguish and makes a deal with God. Hannah is suffering in an undesired and unchosen liminal state of infertility. She is no longer a virgin but is not yet a mother. This liminal state appears to be a source of trauma that makes her weep at the tabernacle as if she were drunk.

My unchosen liminal state was an extended period of singleness. Some would be very happy to extend their singleness; I was not one of them. Moving to an urban area to attend seminary was refreshing because suddenly I was one of many normal single people and the church treated me as any other adult. The people in the small-town church and culture from which I came had acted like my singleness meant I was a college student.

I admit, with Turner, that this liminality was a place of growth and creativity, but it was also a place of deep pain. Some of this pain was due to confusion about the meaning of Christian womanhood,[7] some was due to negative conclusions I made about myself as a single person, and some simply came from the fact that I was in an undesired liminal state full of ambiguity (for which I had not yet developed tolerance). I remember the pain of liminality more than the creativity.

Liminal states can be boring, but more often they are characterized by ambivalence, a mix of opposites: anticipation *and* frustration, grief *and* joy. We anticipate the next, stable state but are frustrated by the process. We are joyful about the future but sad about what we are leaving behind. To get to the next state, we must pass tests and prove ourselves; this makes us anxious and sometimes sleepless. Liminality can be described in one word: vulnerability. Stripped of what once was and not yet clothed with the new, we are bare.

Vulnerability

Even though Brené Brown has prolifically written about, spoken about, podcasted about, and encouraged vulnerability, her efforts are unable to change the fact that many do not like it.[8] A vulnerable person, as conceived of in the popular imagination, is like a ripe peach: easily dented and bruised and then no longer good. We want to avoid being dented and bruised ourselves; we think vulnerability destroys us. But maybe liminal vulnerability is more like clay in the hands of an expert potter. It has its own strength and can be formed and changed into something incredibly beautiful and unique.

Liminal vulnerability is a state of what Dru Johnson calls "scriptlessness." "Scriptlessness can feel like a forest of proliferating paths forward, with no maps. What we experience isn't quite listlessness or discontent; it's either not knowing what to do or feeling saturated with too many options."[9] When left breathless and scriptless, Johnson says, we turn to ritual. But where are the scripted rituals for liminal states? When people feel that they are about to fall into an abyss, how do they find solid ground? What helps us become like the clay and not be destroyed like the peach?

First, psychologist Pauline Boss recommends that "to lower your stress and anxiety during confusing times, increase your tolerance for ambiguity."[10] Boss wrote this in the middle of the COVID-19 pandemic, when the entire world was thrown, against their will, into a liminal state. We suddenly lost our "normal" and did not know when the liminality would end. Boss had long written about ambiguity; she coined the term "ambiguous loss" in 1973 to describe the kind of loss that has no body or casket. The term can describe anything from a 9/11 victim whose body was not recovered to a romantic relationship that has ended.[11] The pandemic's ambiguous losses included the loss of regular rituals, feelings of safety, playdates, freedom, hopes, and more.[12]

Liminality, whether chosen or unchosen, involves ambiguous loss. As much as we want the next state, what we leave behind creates an empty hole. Ritual can help us recognize and grieve those losses, even if we never get closure. (There will be more on closure later in the chapter.)

Nothingness

Nothing seems to happen in liminal states; they are periods of waiting. Like Sarah, who brought Hagar to Abraham, we all find ways of avoiding the nothingness of waiting. When we lose a job, we immediately brush up our resume and check postings. We fill our weekends with activities and our evenings with Netflix bingeing. We fill pauses in conversations with new words, and we fill pauses at the traffic lights by checking our phones. We are allergic to nothingness and emptiness, and we fill it in any way we can.

I found the liminal nothingness of seminary frustrating. Although I was working toward a goal (ministry) and there was a projected end date (graduation), the academic preparation and internship seemed annoying at best. I likened my state to bread dough as it rises. I wasn't yet ready to be baked; rather, I was rising almost imperceptibly, becoming ready for future use.

Traditionally, liminality was intentional nothingness and emptiness. It was only in this state that people could connect with different ways of knowing and growing. The emptiness does not produce immediate visible results, but oh, there is mysterious transformation that comes when we embrace it.[13] William Bridges calls it the "neutral zone," a time of inner reorientation. "It is the phase of the transition process that the modern world pays least attention to. By treating ourselves like appliances that can be unplugged and plugged in again at will, or cars that stop and start with the twist of a key, we have forgotten the importance of fallow time and winter and rests in music. We have abandoned a system of dealing with the neutral zone through ritual, and we have tried to deal with personal change as though it were a matter of simple readjustment."[14]

We have forgotten the forty years Moses spent in exile in Midian before he saw the burning bush (see Acts 7:30). Most of us are not even aware that after St. Paul's conversion and before his first journey in Acts came an interlude of fourteen years (Gal. 2:1; Acts 9:30). He spent the bulk of those years in his hometown, Tarsus, because the apostles sent him away from Jerusalem.[15] The New Testament is virtually empty of stories from Jesus's adolescence and early adulthood, and it records only about four days' worth of events in the fifty days between Jesus's resurrection and Pentecost. The reason the Bible says little about these times might be that nothing much happens that is visual or measurable in the liminal state; no one writes books about the empty liminality. We resist its silence, and we want a map or compass.

But God invites us to liminality every week. God invites us to stop and embrace emptiness every seventh day. Work six days; stop on the seventh. Practicing the Sabbath helps us develop our relationship with creation. The theology of this fourth commandment calls us to answer one question: Do we trust God, or do we trust ourselves? Did the Israelites trust God enough to stop working one day in seven, to refrain from planting one year in seven? Apparently not; only when they were exiled did the land enjoy its Sabbath rest for seventy years (2 Chron. 36:21). When invited to emptiness, they refused; they are a lot like us.

Liminal states create a beautiful *communitas* and a complex mixture of opposite emotions; they make us vulnerable and call us to emptiness and nothingness. Liminal states are not easy, but rituals can help us receive the transformation they offer and embrace them.

Perpetual Liminality

Hannah's infertility ended with the birth of Samuel, the last of the judges to lead Israel. Moses's liminal exile ended with the burning bush, the plagues, and his leading an obstinate people to the promised land. Paul's liminal years ended when Barnabas brought him to Antioch (Acts 11:25–26), from which they soon journeyed together. I ended my liminal singleness with a wedding when I was thirty-nine. While my unchosen liminality lasted longer than I desired, it did come to an end. Had I continued to be single, I may have been considered an old maid or a spinster. Such is our culture's intolerance for ambiguity: we want to put a period at the end of the singleness sentence; its period is either marriage or spinster status. Given the changing demographics of broader American society, in which the unmarried outnumber the married,[16] time will tell whether the church subculture will revisit this sentence-ending period.

Like me, the church likes closure. We like to finish liminality and celebrate its closure with a wedding, a graduation, a baptism. What about cases where there is no closure? I first learned about childhood narcolepsy, a chronic sleep disorder, from a podcast. Mark Labberton interviewed Claire Crisp, whose daughter Mathilda was diagnosed with narcolepsy at the age of three. I had previously thought that narcolepsy simply meant you fell asleep all the time, but that is only part of the disease. In *Waking Mathilda: A Memoir of Childhood Narcolepsy*, Crisp describes other harrowing symptoms, such as hallucinations that are practically inseparable from reality.[17] In the podcast she expresses that she is grateful for healing prayers and believes God can and does heal but that she is not sure that Mathilda will be healed.[18] If she is not, she will be in a perpetual state of liminality, which has inevitable upswings and downswings, with no complete closure.

Hannah's story of infertility-ending birth stands in a long line of similar stories beginning with Sarah, Rebekah, and Rachel and reaching all the way to Mary, the mother of Jesus. Jesus's conception is clearly different but is still vitally connected to Hannah's dropping Samuel off at the temple (1 Sam. 2:24–28). Mary's Magnificat, spoken when she is in her first trimester, echoes the song Hannah sings then (1 Sam. 2:1–10; Luke 1:46–55). The song is wildly revolutionary. It is about God performing mighty deeds, bringing down rulers, lifting up the humble, and sending the rich away. When I read it, I want to say, "Hold on, Mary. You're not even twelve weeks along, Joseph does not know, and he's not the dad; you have trouble ahead." As Mary faces a time of liminality called pregnancy, her Magnificat speaks to the end of an even longer liminality. More than two thousand years later, we still wait for her words to be finally fulfilled.

It seems that the psalmists do this as well: they state that God will do what God has not yet done. The psalmists' cries of "How long, LORD?" (e.g., Ps. 13:1) show that they are in an undesirable liminal state in which they often feel forgotten by God. A full two-thirds of the Psalter, the songbook of the people, are lament psalms, songs that tell God all is not right with the world and ask God to fix the problems. I often wonder what it would be like if two-thirds of the songs we sing in our churches were like that. All but one of the lament psalms resolve with a confession of trust and hope that God will act, just as the Magnificat proclaims God's salvation.[19]

Lament psalms seem to hold two truths in tension: everything is a mess, *and* I will trust God. God's goodness does not solve the mess right now; it is simply an overarching truth. Scholarship is mixed on whether the final resolution portion of most lament psalms is future vows or the current emotional state of the psalmist.[20] Psalms are a dialogue between humans and God, and as such, they may be comparable to a dialogue between humans. Telling another human about my pain or trauma is an initial step in healing.[21] This cathartic release helps us regulate our emotions. Speaking our pain also helps us connect with the "inner voice" of our beliefs and values.[22] When I verbalize my pain and grief with naked honesty, I self-regulate by connecting my pain with what I believe about God. This may be what the psalmist is doing.

Suppressing difficult emotions does not make them disappear; in fact, it may make them more salient. If we try not to think about elephants, our brain will be filled with them. Perhaps the emotional outburst of complaint to God in the context of community (psalms were sung communally) is part of what makes us heal. Maybe expressing sadness with the psalmist will bring us to a more stable state.

The Stories We Tell Ourselves in Liminal States

Frequently, we can ignore the liminality of our lives, but at other times death and illness stare us in the face. Any sickness, no matter how mild, is a reminder of our mortality, a warning that death is coming.[23] Besides being a state of great vulnerability both physically and psychologically, sickness is boring

161

and frustrating.[24] Tish Harrison Warren writes redemptively about her state of illness, "And when I could no longer achieve the things I wanted to, all I was left with was who I am, without adornment, without polish or productivity. Humiliating. But this kind of humiliation humanizes us. Facing our frailty and limitations teaches us how to be human."[25] Learning to be human this way means embracing weakness in a culture that celebrates only strength.

Sociologist Arthur Frank works with those in deep illness, a state of liminality between health and either healing or death. He listens to their stories and has categorized them into three groups: the restitution story, the chaos story, and the quest story.[26] I can illustrate all three stories with reference to the liminality of the pandemic. The restitution story is "There is a global pandemic, they manufacture vaccines, and the world goes back to normal." In this story someone else helps, and the patient is mostly passive.

The chaos story is a personal one for me. My father-in-law dies on March 9, 2020, so my husband travels to Syria to mourn him; and then the borders close him into a country with no US embassy and no functioning airport; and then the whole world shuts down; and then my three-year-old and five-year-old are home with me as I continue working full-time remotely; and then my babysitters stop coming and I can't even go to the grocery store, because my kids touch everything and that's how we think we get sick; and then where I live, New York City, becomes the global epicenter of a pandemic; and then . . . chaos stories suck others into their panicky vortex.

My quest story goes like this: We journey through the pandemic; it's hard and awful, and we are isolated; then the vaccines come. When we are fully vaccinated, we invite some of our closest friends over for a meal. We have hardly eaten with anyone besides one another for more than a year. Before dessert, we head downstairs to light candles. We say the names of

162

those who have died, and we place a candle for each in black sand. Then we enumerate the other losses, placing their candles in blue sand. Our growth candles go in green sand, and our joys go in red sand. The deaths burn out first, and then the joys tower over and lean toward all the others. We say, "The LORD gives, and the LORD takes away. Blessed be the name of the LORD" (Job 1:21 CSB), and we pray. We know there will be more losses, so we go home with a pot containing mixed-colored sand and more candles to burn when those losses come. We find meaning in something we nevertheless wish had never happened.

Frank is careful not to judge the stories or try to move people from one type of story to another; he believes they own their stories, and they get to tell them. When I read the stories, though, I am attracted to the quest story. It seems to connect to the Psalms, and I think Pauline Boss would recommend it. She states that one way to resilience is finding meaning.[27] My quest story shows that while I moved to another stage in pandemic life, the pandemic was far from over. Marking the end of my no-vaccination stage helped me continue in the pandemic's liminal ambiguity. It also gave me a ritual to practice when I face challenges in the ambiguity. Thinking about the pandemic in terms of a quest helps me acknowledge gains along the liminal pathway. My quest story and ritual did not celebrate closure, and Boss would say that closure is a myth, an illusion. This truth has given me a great deal of freedom.

I suppose telling a quest story is easier when the end is what we want. Hannah can sing about her baby Samuel and perhaps see the years of anguish as bringing her to this place of motherhood. While Boss encourages us to find meaning as a path through ambiguity, some losses never make sense, "so naming them 'meaningless' becomes their meaning."[28] Kate Bowler, diagnosed with aggressive cancer in the prime of her life, writes about the Christian push for the quest story and positive meaning in her memoir, *Everything Happens for a Reason and Other Lies I've Loved.*[29] Appendix 1 of her book lists many unhelpful comments people make to those who are experiencing terrible times; the comments prescribe meaning, as with the line "Everything happens for a reason." We would do better to remember that the sufferer may be in the midst of a chaos story and that our job is to listen, not prescribe meaning.

The end of my chaos story is that my husband came home on a repatriation flight eight and a half weeks later. My body and mind took a long time to process everything, and I did a ritual that I thought would bring closure. My friend said that I was a warrior princess when he was gone, so I bought a wire crown and retrieved some ribbon we had used in our wedding. On that ribbon I wrote out all that my boys and I did, the number of hikes, tick bites, video calls, and more, ending with "one family finally together." I wound that around the wire crown, wept, and thought I had closure. Whenever I think about that time, however, I still feel the chaos. I thought maybe I had not done enough to process, but Boss encourages me when she says there is no absolute end in our losses.[30] That time of my life is still sometimes painful, and that is okay. I also think that time was meaningless.

Embracing Liminality

So, how do we increase our tolerance for our own and others' liminal ambiguity? First, we must let go of what once was and embrace the liminal state. In March 2020 we thought that COVID-19 would shut down the world for two weeks and then we would get back to normal. After a time, most of us realized there was no going back; instead of a return to normal, we began to embrace the ambiguous and unformed future as it unfolded. Letting go of what once was enabled us to turn and embrace the future. Letting go is explained in the chapter on ends and the chapter on beginnings; ritual helps us.

Refusing to recognize liminal ambiguity does not make it any less real. In the same way that embracing sadness leads us to greater happiness, embracing ambiguity can lead to greater clarity. It may take a while, but that is our journey.

We see our friends and ourselves in a liminal place, and we want to "solve" liminality by moving to a more stable state. The church prays for healing for those with chronic illness, prays for jobs for the unemployed, prays for spouses for the single. These prayers are usually well intentioned and kind. My nephew was born with a genetic heart defect; that is why he had open-heart surgery when he was four days old and again when he was three years old. His heart still has issues. He is now eighteen, but when he was young, I shared with my sister that I was continually praying for his healing. She thanked me and told me that she prayed for other things. You see, I was seeing my nephew mainly through the lens of his illness. I did not have the broader picture of him and his needs that a parent would.

I am not suggesting that we stop praying for healing, jobs, and spouses. Rather, I am suggesting that we not see healing, jobs, and spouses as the only or primary way God works in our lives. I am suggesting that the lenses by which we view others not be their illness, unemployment, singleness, or other state of apparent lack. When Barbara Newman speaks about universal design for worship, she points out that we are each a puzzle piece, a mix of what we are good at and what we struggle with. Any given piece is incomplete on its own without the whole puzzle. We lose sight of the beautiful picture our pieces create together when we focus primarily on where people struggle.[31] Perhaps our job as a church is not to solve what we perceive as problems; perhaps it is to become comfortable with others' liminal ambiguity and journey together.

Embracing liminality also means increasing our tolerance for ambiguity. Boss has six guidelines for how to increase resilience in times of ambiguous loss, three of which are applicable to times of liminality. She is careful to note that increasing resilience should never take the place of necessary systemic change. Systemic racism can cause people of color to be in a perpetual state of feeling unsafe. Rather than helping people embrace a liminal lack of safety, we must work for systemic change.

When liminal ambiguity is not attached to faulty systems, however, ritual can help people increase resilience. Boss recommends six actions, in no particular order: find meaning, adjust mastery, reconstruct identity, discover new hope, revise attachment, and normalize ambivalence.[32] While many often begin with seeking meaning, it is not necessary to begin there. One can begin by normalizing ambivalence.[33] We noted that liminal states are characterized by ambivalence, a mix of opposite emotions at the same time. Ambivalence feels confusing, and we want to reject it in order to experience only emotions that feel good. Our best bet for resilience, however, is to normalize it. For engaged people, feeling utter joy and also sheer terror of the future is good and normal. Ambivalence happens when we are liminal; normalizing the ambivalence can free us and increase our resilience.

We can also adjust mastery, or realize what we cannot control, which, honestly, is most things.[34] Often, we have a false notion of our ability to control our lives, so when hardships come, we have a hard time being resilient; we are shocked that bad things happen, especially when we have done everything we can to prevent the bad. Our best path toward resilience is releasing what we cannot control and embracing what we can.

As a college professor I hear many more breakup stories than engagement ones. Some of the breakups really send the students reeling. Their grades suffer, and they do not know how to be resilient in this state of significant ambiguous loss. I always ask about their personal health—sleep, diet, and exercise. Usually, these areas are suffering. My advice is always to eat three healthy meals a day, exercise at least three times a week, try to get eight hours of sleep, and go to the college counseling center for free help. In times of loss, we cannot master the grief, but we can at least approach mastery of areas that are in our control.

Boss also recommends building resilience in times of loss by reconstructing identity. She writes of the loss of her husband and the fact that widowhood doesn't really fit her yet; she loved being a wife so much that letting go of that identity is a process.[35] Possibly the hardest part about liminal ambiguity is this: we are no longer who we were, but we are not yet who we will be. What used to define us no longer does, and our future is unclear. We cannot reconstruct without letting go, but perpetual liminality requires that we become comfortable with simply being. Perhaps we lose our previous career or our health and we are simply a frail human, deeply loved by God.

Ritually Flying Flags

While we float through this liminal life, we ritually mark beginnings and ends, but the long middles are often left both unritualized and unrecognized. As such, we avoid and ignore ambiguity rather than increase our tolerance for it. Then, when liminal ambiguity smacks us in the face, we feel we are about to sink. The journey across the ocean is long, and when we cannot see land, we need signs to help us keep going.

Merritt Tierce writes that when ships have lost all other forms of communication, they fly nautical flags.[36] Many ships have them in case of emergency; there are forty different flags that have meaning both by themselves and in combination with others. According to the International Code of Signals, a flag

167

with a black circle in a yellow background next to a vertically striped red, white, and blue flag means "I am on fire." A red-diamond flag next to a square flag containing a yellow and a red triangle means "I will keep close to you."[37]

Tierce states, "I wish we could fly such flags, we humans, ships unto ourselves, to communicate our states of balm or damage, our current headings, our desires and lacks. Maybe my friend's radio has gone out, but at least he could fly his small I-am-suffering-on-this-sunny-day flag and I could raise my I-will-take-a-walk-with-you-and-listen flag. We could see each other, understand, and act, without having to say all the words."[38]

It is hard to find words for difficult liminal states let alone articulate our liminality in casual conversations by the water cooler. Patterned signals communicate clearly and quickly. Individual rituals of liminality fly the medium-sized this-is-hard-but-I-will-continue-and-trust flag. Corporate rituals of liminality raise large we-journey-with-you-and-you-are-valuable flags and allow those in the liminal state to fly their small the-ambiguity-is-overwhelming flag or the medium-sized today-I-feel-hopeful flag. We speak thus, with and without words.

Right-Now Ritual: Liminal Times

Liminality brings feelings of instability; finding our moorings and our grounding is challenging. Julian of Norwich is famous for writing what Jesus said to her: "All shall be well, and all shall be well, and all manner of things shall be well."[39] While I appreciate this sentiment and do believe it overall, I also know we face tragedies and difficult, destabilizing experiences. It is hard to trust God in these times, but this ritual can help. The key progression is complaint to God, accessing physical stability, paying attention to current stability and provision, and declaring trust in God.

Liminal Times

Breathe deeply and bring yourself into the present moment.

Out loud and to God, state the ambiguity that is troubling you. It can be as simple as "God, I have lost what once was, and I do not know what is next."

Put both feet solidly on the floor and press them down. Concentrate on the feeling of stability and grounding this brings. Bring to mind several examples of stable elements in your life, such as food, housing, relationships, a salary. Observe these elements one by one, seeking to stand on them with your feet as you press down.

Hold a glass of water. As you hold it, note the stability and solid nature of the cup. Ponder the gift of having access to clean water, and remind yourself that water sustains your life and body. Thank God for the gift of water.

Drink the water and state your trust in God as provider. "Lord, you have given me this water to sustain me; I trust that you will provide what I need." *You may state this many times at once or several times each day.*

Breathe deeply and allow trust in God to permeate your being.

Right-Now Ritual: Empowerment in the Middle of Any Task

As I faced challenges in the middle of writing, I did this ritual. It offers a reset and empowerment when they are needed. The key progression is movement, comfort, receiving Holy Spirit empowerment, and anointing.

Empowerment in the Middle of Any Task

Change your location. Go outside, if possible, and move, becoming aware of your body. I do this while walking. Allow the conflicting or ambivalent feelings to exist, and treat yourself as you would a friend, comforting yourself. Perhaps put your hand on your chest and say, "Sorry, friend." Keep doing this until you feel comforted.

Keep moving and feel the air or wind on your face. Raise your head to breathe it in, and put your shoulders back (some call this a "power pose").[40] *Pray these words:* "Lord I receive the wind of your Holy Spirit to empower me for the task you have placed before me. Fill me." *Breathe in deeply.*

Finally, anoint whatever part of your body is involved in this task with oil and ask God to empower it or them to keep going and accomplish what God desires. Breathe in one more time, pray, and go back to the task.

At-Church Ritual: Marking the Liminal State

The journey of healing physically, finding a spouse or job, or moving toward another goal can be long and difficult. This ritual is intended to mark the journey toward the goal. The key progression is naming losses and letting go, naming the gains and marking the journey, and blessing.

Marking the Liminal State

Preparation

Minister or leader of the small group offers an open invitation to anyone who is challenged by their liminal state. Ideally, the ritual will be repeated once a year. Participants will familiarize themselves with their parts in the ritual in advance and will choose a sponsor who will stand with and listen to their declarations; they will also prepare the following:

- A written list or symbol of the losses they have experienced in the past year (they will leave this at the altar, and these losses should have to do with the liminal state).
- A modifiable symbol for the journey, such as a necklace that increases by a special bead each year or a wooden

frame that is notched each year and into which a new
photo is placed each year.

· A written list of their gains in the past year, including any
that are not clearly related to the liminal state (e.g., a promotion at work in the midst of a chronic illness, or a new
medication that is effective).

The Ritual

*If the ritual takes place in church, those honoring their liminal state
are at the altar, facing the minister, with their sponsor next to them.
A container is available for what participants are releasing. If the
ritual is done in a small group, the setup is chosen according to
what best fits the space.*

Leader: Liminality is a time of being betwixt and between,
being no longer who we were and not yet what we will be, being
no longer where we were and not yet where we will be. While all
of life is liminal, certain types of liminality are more challenging
than others. Today, we honor those in long, challenging liminality; we do not seek to "solve" their liminal state, but we honor
it and walk alongside them. *Leader prayers extemporaneously.*
Along this past year's journey there has been loss. We invite the
participants to name their losses and release them.

Participants: *They hold the list or symbol of losses and name
the losses to their sponsor or the group, depending on their preference. Then they place the list or symbol in the loss container.*

Leader: (*After making an extemporaneous prayer of release*)
Along this past year's journey there has been gain. We invite the
participants to name their gains and symbolize them.

*Participants hold the symbol of gain; name the gains to the
sponsor or group, depending on their preference; and do the
symbolic act (e.g., put the bead on the necklace, notch the wooden
frame and put in the current photo).*

*Leader gives an extemporaneous prayer of blessing on the
liminal journey, being careful not to "solve" the liminality.*

8

Beginnings

JESUS'S MINISTRY BEGINS WITH A RITUAL. It is a ritual John the Baptist thinks is unnecessary for him, but Jesus does it "to fulfill all righteousness" (Matt. 3:15). Jesus is baptized. Baptism is not uncommon for someone in the first century. Individuals are baptized into the name of the one they follow. John's baptism is different, however, as it is a baptism of repentance, not simply a baptism as a teacher's disciple. When Jesus comes up out of the water, his identity is confirmed by God: "This is my Son, whom I love; with him I am well pleased" (v. 17). After this identity confirmation that comes through ritual, Jesus begins to teach, heal, and deliver.

Our baptisms are also intended to offer identity to the baptized. Christian traditions baptize people who are new to the faith;[1] the ritual is intended to allow new believers to identify with Christ's death and resurrection as well as to identify as full members of a community of faith, as Christians. Baptism is the ritual gateway for ministry, the Eucharist, and more.

Christians like to celebrate beginnings and often do so with ritual. We celebrate life's beginning with a baby dedication or baptism, the beginning of a marriage with a wedding, the beginning of ministry with ordination. We may disenfranchise ends and hurry or ignore middles, but many beginnings are enfranchised and celebrated and continue to be recognized by the community after the event. We like to talk about beginnings and avoid conversations about ends or middles. "How is married life?" is a common question for quite a while after the wedding, while "How is widowhood?" and "How is unemployment?" are quite rare. At commencement the conversation centers on "What is next?" more than "What do you miss about high school?"

Beginnings are identity-forming foundations for the future. We always look back on the beginning to remind us of who we are and, at times, *whose* we are. We take photos, frame them, and put them on a wall or send them to our loved ones. Beginnings are declarations: you are a wife, you are a husband, you are a Christian, you are a graduate, you are a reverend. We love beginnings and the joy and transformation of the declaration.

While sources abound on ending well or figuring out liminal states, less is available for beginnings in general. We think we do it well, and in many senses we do. The commonality of ritual and community recognition for beginnings help us begin well. Thus, this will be the shortest chapter of part 3.

It is also the shortest chapter because transformational beginning rituals are built on powerful ends and middles. That is to say, as we recognize ends and middles through ritual, beginnings become more easily navigable. As we let go of previous identity markers at ends or middles, we have space for the new identity markers of beginnings.

While we embrace beginnings, we are still surprised at their inherent challenges. "Beginnings are meant to be celebrated," say our rituals that present the excitement, joy, and anticipation of a beginning. Perhaps it is time also to recognize other aspects

174

of beginnings. Once again, a journey motif is helpful here; rituals are markers on the journey that show where we are.

Arrival Fallacy

Most people believe the prevailing idea that the beginning is really the arrival. Once we have achieved the goal of a wedding, a baby, our own business, or retirement, we will then live "happily ever after." The problem comes when the dream life we imaginatively curated when we were moving toward the goal is not what the accomplishment actually looks like. It is often boring, mundane, or even sad. It is joyful and exciting too, just not all the time. Our media portrays beginnings in the same way we fantasize about them, and we seldom want to dispel others' illusions about the joy of marriage, children, and self-employment. The result is that when we experience the challenges of these great beginnings, we are surprised. Yes, beginnings are to be celebrated and are great and wonderful and challenging and hard work all at the same time. Here being aware of arrival fallacy is helpful.

Arrival fallacy is the idea that once we get the beginning we want (e.g., a house, a new job, a baby, a wedding), we will finally be happy and fulfilled and will never want again. Arrival, however, seldom meets our expectations. We are left with a sense of anticlimax, and then we feel guilty because the dream does not feel as we imagined it would feel.[2] We judge ourselves and hide our continued feelings of lack or sadness. Part of the problem is that the rituals we use to mark beginnings tend to acknowledge only the good. Beginnings, indeed, can bring a great deal of good. Yet like ends and middles, they are characterized by complex emotions that include fear and anxiety. Moreover, they can be unpredictable, slow, and integrated with the past, and self-doubt may accompany hope.

Characteristics of Beginnings

Anxiety and Hope

The Germans say, "Every beginning is difficult,"[3] and William Bridges writes, "New beginnings are accessible to everyone, and everyone has trouble with them."[4] "The beginnings of all human undertakings are untidy," writes English novelist John Galsworthy.[5] Beginning a marriage or new job is delightful, hope-filled, and challenging. We like safety, and any change, no matter how good, reveals inner resistance, fear, and anxiety.[6] A promotion or new job involves training and responsibility that might be intimidating.[7] Attending college away from home can cause mild to severe anxiety.[8] Beginnings are complex.

Beginning a new personal endeavor often brings out impostor phenomenon, which is the feeling that one does not belong despite evidence that one does.[9] Bridges states he experiences this self-doubt whenever he begins a project with a new company; he counters it with a personal reminder that he is offering something valuable.[10] Because ritual names something, it can prove helpful when people encounter the self-doubt of a new beginning. When I wonder about my skills as a wife or a professor, I remind myself that it was not by accident that I got married or received a PhD. Neither beginning was merely a gift that had no requirements for me. My husband knew whom he was marrying when he said, "I do," and I spent five years proving myself in order to earn the PhD. I remember my name change to Mrs. and Dr., and my intentional recall of that ritual act affirms my identity.

Professor and Jesuit priest Peter Clark finds self-doubt in a beginning we seldom commemorate: that of palliative care.[11] At the beginning of palliative care, providers shift from fighting disease to making patients comfortable as the disease ends their lives. It is both an end and a beginning. Patients have two options: "First, the patient can be overwhelmed by the fear of suffering and death, which can result in feelings of abandonment and despair. Second, the patient can, with the support of loved ones, accept the inevitability of suffering and death and grow in his or her dependence upon others and God."[12] Clark invented a beautiful "Rite of Christian Commitment to the Terminally Ill." The rite intends to alleviate patients' fear and anxiety and transform the relationship with their family or caregivers.[13] Suffering and death allow people to participate in the paschal mystery, and Christians have always seen them as part of redemption. Furthermore, a theology of dependence argues that humans are always dependent on God and others, as much as they might try to ignore it.[14] Clark's rite seeks to transform relationships through word and deed and to focus on hope rather than anxiety at this important beginning, though the hope rests not in this life. Ritualizing this change reveals the interconnectedness of ends, beginnings, and middles, as this change is all three: it is the end of fighting and the beginning of palliative care, and it stands between health and death.

Usually, in beginnings our hope is in this life. We move to a new house, start a master's program, or open a business, hoping for and seeking future good in these beginnings.[15] Our rituals focus on hope, but I wonder if they can also recognize the fear, anxiety, and resistance that exist in these beginnings.

Unpredictable and Slow

I know someone who decided he was ready for marriage. He had completed his education and landed a steady job, and now he sought a life partner. A year later I attended his wedding as he marked the beginning of married life. I, on the other hand, decided I was ready for marriage in the middle of my undergraduate degree, but my wedding bells did not chime until more than eighteen years later. I watched a friend quit a good job with no other job in sight; two months later he began his new job. I have also watched others remain unemployed for months to years. Beginnings are unpredictable and often slow.

I was awarded my PhD two weeks before I took students on an early-Christian-history trip to Syria. I had a strange feeling that something life-altering would happen on the trip, so I made sure to call all my relatives before I left in case I died. I was right in sensing that my life would be altered on the trip, but it was not death that awaited. I met the man I would marry there. Who could have predicted that?

There is no clear checklist to complete or map to follow that measures when we are ready for a beginning, as much as we might desire it. Bridges finds beginnings intuitive and argues that opportunities arise when we are ready for them because of our work in the neutral zone.[16] Unfortunately for me, this sounds a little like a well-meaning piece of advice I received: "When you are fully satisfied with Christ alone, then you will find your husband." This raises all sorts of theological red flags, not the least of which is the assumption that a spouse is the reward for being faithful to Jesus when Jesus himself was single. Still, it connects with Bridges's idea that we ready ourselves in the neutral zone for the beginning. He is encouraging us to keep walking the path of the neutral zone until there is a new beginning, however long that might take. He also encourages us not to think that measuring our progress will make the beginning come sooner.

I agree with Bridges about continuing neutral zone work as we anticipate new beginnings, but I add that reality can be messier. We know stories of relationships that follow on the heels of breakups but that lead to marriage, or of a happily employed person taking a new job that leads to great success. Each life journey is individual, though one can discern general patterns. The general pattern here is that beginnings are unpredictable and our work in the neutral zone is important. We think everything should start when we want it to; this is often not the case.[17]

In lifespan development, retirement is also called reinvention, and Judith McCoyd, Jeanne Koller, and Carolyn Walter argue it is a journey of fits and starts.[18] Even though a person may have ritually begun their retirement/reinvention with some sort of party or ceremony, the beginning is still slow. It takes time to adjust to a significant alteration of one's roles, relationships, routines, and assumptions. Beginnings are unpredictable and slow.

We can certainly see this in 1–2 Samuel in David's beginning as king. His father takes him from the fields, he meets Samuel, and Samuel anoints him king, performing the ritual that sets someone apart with oil, the symbol of the Holy Spirit. This is the beginning, but David's kingship is not fulfilled for years. His identity is changed, but his wife Michal helps him flee Saul, and he spends years hiding from Saul in the desert and with the Philistines. Only after a gruesome battle and Saul's and Jonathan's death does David take the throne. Even then, he still must depose Saul's offspring. We like to think beginnings are not like that, but they often are.

Connected to the Past

In chapter 6, I explained that ends offer continuing bonds with the past; beginnings are also connected with the past in an empowering way. This truth was depicted for me when my sister and her husband lit the unity candle at their wedding. For those unfamiliar with this symbolic action, at the beginning of the wedding rite, parents light individual tapers that represent the life of the bride and groom. After the vows, the bride and groom bring their tapers together to light the unity candle and then blow out their tapers, representing their unity. My sister's officiant asked them to leave their tapers burning rather than blow them out. While weddings do unite two people in one flesh, the two also remain individuals with distinct gifts and callings.

It is true that a wife or husband is different from a single person, but a significant connection to the person they have always been still exists. Bridges looks at beginnings as a reintegration of identity—that is, an integration of who the person was before and who the person has become. Yes, there are new aspects of the person, but many aspects of who the person was remain and can still be celebrated.

Embracing Beginnings

So, how do we transform the way we embrace beginnings? Christianity already recognizes that rituals help us begin; how can we enhance existing rituals and create new ones that are even more helpful?

The obvious answer is to create rituals that name the complexities that the new beginning will offer. I cringe a little when I write this. I long for celebrations that are only about the good. I long for a world without sin, for pure excitement without anxiety, for pure joy without sadness, and for pure anticipation without fear. My longing for purity is based, however, more in "happily ever after" fairy tales than in the world in which I live. There is no beginning without an ending, no excitement without anxiety, and no anticipation without fear. Good and bad constantly coexist. To deny that is to deny reality. To the extent that rituals create an alternative world, rituals must also be grounded in this world of coexisting opposites. How can our rituals both recognize that tension and also, particularly for beginnings, focus on identity formation for the future? Let us consider symbols and identity formation in beginnings.

Chapter 3 explored the way in which gang initiations not only act for the initiate but also remind all members of their

own initiation and their shared affiliation. In short, they point
to identity. I wonder if we can do this for beginnings too. I
attended a baptism at an Episcopal church, and rather than
simply watch a stranger be baptized, we were invited to take
part in the ritual. We all renounced the devil, and we all declared allegiance to Christ. It was powerful. Many sacramental churches invite those present to remember their baptism
by prayerfully touching the blessed baptismal water. In the
baptismal renewal that I offer to my classes, I put blessed
water on their foreheads, stating, "May the Holy Spirit, who
has begun a good work in you, direct and uphold you in the
service of Christ and his kingdom. Amen."[19] This can be done
for all who attend a baptism; it reminds them of their own
identity as a Christian as they participate in the baptism of
another.

Baptisms, weddings, and commencements have identity-
forming symbols that are helpful for people when they are
faced with the unpredictability, slowness, and self-doubt of
the life that follows. Baptized persons often receive a cross to
wear around their neck at all times, rings are symbols of the
marriage union, and a diploma states that the degree is earned
and honors the completed work. When living as a Christian
is challenging, we can hold the cross and remember our identity and the ritual that claimed it; when marriage has ups and
downs, we can twist the ring and remember our vows; when
impostor phenomenon raises its ugly head, academics can
look at the diplomas on their office wall and remind themselves of who they are. And we would be more likely to do
this if our beginning rituals taught us that the symbol is not
just for the ritual but is also for strength and encouragement
when the state we have entered, the state that the beginning
ritual celebrates, feels different than it does on the day of the
ritual.

At-Church Ritual: Beginning the School Year

Many families take photos on the first day of school, and many churches perform the "Blessing of Backpacks." Students begin new classes, and sometimes teachers begin working in a new location. This ritual is meant to bless and empower students and teachers as they begin.[20] It may also be adapted for use when a person experiences another beginning, such as a new job. The key progression is anointing and blessing.

Beginning the School Year

Preparation

All teachers and all students bring their backpacks (or other bags) and the gear they will use to accomplish their tasks. These are placed in the front of the church.

The church purchases stones with words like "faith," "believe," or "grace" on them. Holy water and anointing oil may be used. The ritual should come at the end of the worship service.

The Ritual

All students (whatever age) and teachers stand together in the front of the church, facing the leader.

Leader extemporaneously states the purpose of the ritual, which is to honor the beginning that these people are about to make. Leader then invites each participant to state their name and where and what they will begin—for example, "My name is Amy Davis Abdallah, and I will begin teaching practical theology and worship at Alliance University."

Leader: (*Consecrates the backpacks while sprinkling holy water on them, saying these words*) I consecrate these bags and their contents for holy use by the women, men, girls, and boys here in the name of the Father, Son, and Holy Spirit.

Leader anoints each person with oil, making the sign of the cross, and gives them a stone, saying, "I anoint you with the power of the Holy Spirit for this beginning in the name of the Father, Son, and Holy Spirit."

Congregation: (*Extending their hands in blessing to the participants*) Beginning does not mean you have arrived. This beginning may be filled with both anxiety and hope as well as other conflicting feelings; it is new but still connected to your past, and it may progress more slowly than you would like. But we say it is good. We are with you in this beginning, and we bless it. We have given you a stone as a reminder that we are with you and a symbol to hold in prayer when you are faced with challenges.

Leader gives an extemporaneous prayer of blessing. Volunteers, perhaps using an instant camera, take a photo of each participant with their backpack and stone and give the photo to them.

Reflections on Beginning Rituals

The following is intended as a reflection for the evaluation and change of existing beginning rituals (for individuals or small groups). The rituals may vary, but two common ones to evaluate would be a baptism and a wedding. These recommendations are best used alongside the "Reflections on Rituals' Transformational Power" section in chapter 5.

1. Begin with prayer, asking for God's wisdom in this exercise.
2. Reflect on the ritual using the following questions:
   - Have we pastored those who are beginning through the end and middle that preceded this beginning? How? Has this progress been ritualized? What can we do to more clearly honor the ends and middles that precede the momentous beginning?
   - How does the ritual acknowledge the various aspects of beginnings, including arrival fallacy, anxiety and

hope, the slowness of beginnings, and connection to the past? Does the acknowledgment come through word, action, or a physical symbol? If not, what can we do to convey the complexity of beginnings?

- Does this ritual offer a clear identity and declaration for the individuals involved? How does it encourage them to remember the beginning when they doubt?

- How does the ritual allow all those present to reflect on their shared identity? For example, how does a baptism invite all of those present who have been baptized to remember their shared identity as baptized Christians? How does a wedding invite all married attenders to remember their shared identity as married people? The answer to the latter question may be complex, given that single individuals, widows, widowers, and divorcees are in attendance. Still, the question deserves reflection.

3. Create an action plan for ritual change.

4. End in prayer.

Conclusion

Making Ritual Matter

My friend is leaving a place she gave her heart and soul to for twenty years. Her final year brought challenges that caused her to look elsewhere and left a bad taste in her mouth. As she transitions to a new position, she has all the contradictory emotions of ends, middles, and beginnings, is trying to make room to express them, and has no real map for doing so.

I'm offering her support through ritual action. The ritual will acknowledge the end's losses and empower her beginning. She will write down what has caused the negative feelings, read what she has written to a small group of friends around a firepit, declare that she is letting go, and burn the paper. Then, to acknowledge continuing bonds, she will also state the good that came from those twenty years, including how she was transformed. After she states her hopes for the new position, we will give her a necklace with a symbol of identity and newness and offer prayers of blessing for this beginning. I hope it will transform her understanding of the past and empower her continuing journey.

I think it will be powerful. It pays attention to this step on her journey, has the purpose of transformation, and requires community investment. It makes room for ambivalent emotions, allows her to make meaning, incorporates the symbolic act of burning, and endows her with a symbol of empowerment. If she encounters self-doubt, she can touch her necklace and remind herself of the blessings we gave and the community support she has. Her community enfranchises her loss and celebrates her gain.

I dream of communities characterized by rituals like this. If I experience a painful-joyful transition like hers in the future, I hope my community will offer a ritual. I know they would celebrate the new, but would they also help me say goodbye to the old?

I dream of churches and other communities that acknowledge and grieve disenfranchised loss through ritual. We can ritualize on our own, yes, but how beautiful and how much more powerful would it be in community!

My biggest dream concerns the oft-ignored liminality. When a woman anxiously begins a new medication regimen to fight her cancer, how can her community alleviate her anxiety through ritual? When a man's singleness journey lasts longer than he likes, how do we help him mark stops on his journey? When individuals face long-term unemployment, how do we ritually acknowledge their continuing value?

We can do this.

Doing so can be as simple as adopting a power pose and saying, "Holy Spirit, you've got me," before taking the medication each time; close friends can do the same pose and declaration on her behalf every day.

It can be a ritual burning with friends; it can be a service, led by a minister, that recognizes a miscarriage.

It can be as complex as a yearlong rite of passage called *Woman*.

The simplicity or complexity does not matter; I simply dream of us ritualizing and thus being transformed and offering transformation. Rituals matter—for you and for me and for us.

To make a right end of our time together, I invite you to perform a simple right-now ritual. As written, it involves hands and feet; feel free to choose another body part or physical object.

> Place your feet solidly on the floor, get comfortable in your seat, and close your eyes. Pray that God would consecrate these next moments. Hold your hands, palms up, in a posture of receiving. Figuratively place in your left hand anything from this book that was not helpful and that you need to let go. When you are ready, turn your hand over and declare, "I let it go." Figuratively place in your right hand the good from this book, remembering specific portions you want to take with you. When you have placed all these things there, take your right hand and bring it to your heart, praying, "Lord, keep this with me." You may want to continue in prayer or choose a first step for ritualizing.

Imagine me raising my hands in blessing as I leave you with Paul's exhortation and benediction from Philippians: "Whatever you have learned or received or heard from me, or seen in me—put it into practice. And the God of peace will be with you" (Phil. 4:9).

Exploring Our Sources

My understanding of the following sources is that they were written for the church, and as we are members of the church, they are available for our use to the glory of God. Not all will understand the sources this way. It may even be that these sources were written with a particular denomination in mind, but there is no reason why they must be limited to that denomination. I see the vast history of written and performed liturgies as amazing sources that can help us ritualize. In this appendix I will describe several sources and give hints for using them well.

Hints for Effective Source Use

When you begin to explore these sources, they might feel overwhelming. My purpose below is to help you figure out which sources to use and how best to use them. I will begin with overall recommendations.

Cite Your Sources

In the divorce ritual in chapter 6, I originally included af-firmations at the end, some of which I found in an online rite. Unfortunately, I did not write which were mine or where I got the others, so I had to delete them all. It was a loss for the ritual, and I regret not including citations. Some sources are easier to cite than others. Books are easy; when I use the Book of Common Prayer, I often simply write the title of the prayer or liturgy and put "BCP" in parentheses. When I use internet sources, I need more information. Citing the sources up front makes for less headache if you need to find them later.

Take Your Time

The invention of powerful rituals is not to be hurried. The sources are rich and varied; take time to peruse the sources to see the different ways they address needs. If, for example, you like the Orthodox prayer for miscarriage, use it only after prayerful pondering. Analyze the prayer, delineate what it does, and ask whether it meets the needs of those whom you serve. What might be removed from the prayer, and what might be added for the particular situation? Then consult chapter 5 to nurture the greatest possible transformation.

Work with Others

We have blind spots. Working with others with different ex-pertise aids our ability to create more transformational rituals. Further, it is important to get buy-in from those whom the ritual will serve. Are they comfortable with the words, actions, and symbols of the ritual?

Take Risks and Be Creative

Act, and invite others to act, in a way that is new and dif-ferent, even challenging. Change the words; delete some and add others. The actions that accompany the words from the sources can be distinct to your particular context. Stimulate all the senses, involve bodies, and act in a memorable way. Brainstorm; welcome *all* ideas, and then choose the best. This can be quite fun.

Recommended Sources

Every Moment Holy, Volumes 1 and 2[1]

Though these two beautiful books contain written rituals without rubrics or symbols, I still recommend them as sources to which one might add actions and symbols. The prayers and liturgies are often long and detailed, which makes them useful for adapting to particular situations.

Volume 1 covers almost everything we do, from washing windows to having a morning coffee to facing death. Douglas McKelvey divides prayers into categories like labor and vocation, creation and recreation, blessing and celebration, petition and provision, sorrow and lament, and liturgies of the moment. If one ever lacks words for a particular action or time, McKelvey provides them. While volume 1 contains one prayer for death and grieving, volume 2 is titled *Death, Grief, and Hope* and provides prayers for this journey. Many of the prayers are for individual use and for the moment, yet all can be edited or adapted for groups or specific moments.

The Book of Common Prayer[2]

The Book of Common Prayer was first written and compiled by Thomas Cranmer during the Reformation in Britain. It has since been updated and revised multiple times. The Episcopal Church's 1979 edition contains guidelines for all the services in the denomination and is freely available online. The theology of the book is Protestant, though not every Protestant Christian agrees with all of it. It is worth perusal. The most helpful sections for our purposes would be "Pastoral Offices" and "Episcopal Services."

Pastoral offices include the rite of reconciliation, which I adapted for use in the example ritual for divorce. The rite helped conceptualize reconciliation in order that I might offer it to my friend. The ritual called "Thanksgiving for the Birth or Adoption of a Child" brings tears to my eyes, as I imagine its beauty and impact in the middle of a Sunday service. Also, there are the marriage rite, commitment to Christian service, prayers for the sick, and burial services.

Episcopal services involve consecrating people for holy office and consecrating places for holy use. They could easily be adapted for the consecration of people to various different positions of service to God and even for home blessings. I often state that my liturgical heart, so to speak, is Anglican, so I love this book.

Roman Catholic and Orthodox Prayers

While Roman Catholicism and Orthodoxy are quite distinct from one another, we will group them together here as non-Protestant Christian traditions. Protestantism would not exist except for the fifteen hundred years of Christianity that preceded it; we disagree with some aspects of their practice, but we also agree on key theological ideas like Christ, the Trinity, and salvation.

Many Roman Catholic prayers exist, but they need theological editing as well as language updating. There is a list available online (www.catholic.org/prayers/), though it can be difficult to navigate easily. I find Orthodox prayers easier to navigate and full of biblical themes; I also find they might need some language adaptation but generally need less theological editing. There are several different Orthodox traditions; the primary ones, for our purposes, are Greek, Antiochian,[3] and the Orthodox Church in America (OCA). The Orthodox prayers are very trinitarian and connected to history. A Greek parish in Massachusetts has published an online prayer book, and their sections "Family Prayers," "Prayers in Time of Illness," "Prayers in Time of Trouble," "General Prayers," and "Prayers for Study" are most helpful.[4] The prayers for the dead given later in the book include a beautiful prayer after miscarriage, and the OCA prayers include a service for miscarriage or stillbirth.[5] The Antiochian occasional prayers contain several distinct ones: the prayer of married persons, single persons, and children. They might be helpful for a vow renewal or a service that honors long singleness. In general the subjects of these prayers can act as jumping-off points for any rite on the topic.[6]

The Internet and Other Traditions

The internet is a source for insightful and thoughtful rituals. When I look for rites for women, however, I also find a great deal of strange material. While Christian rites for women are full of words, non-Christian ones are full of symbols involving goddesses, the moon, and flowering. Still, even though Christians might be tempted to dismiss these out of hand, they might read these rituals in the hopes of identifying aspects of human life and the human soul that cry out for a specific ritual. In chapter 4, I mentioned Gordon Dalbey's adaptation of a Nigerian rite of passage. When he describes the ritual, he notes that the Nigerians were calling on a spirit who is not the Christian God. This did not cause him to dismiss the rite altogether; rather, he saw calling into manhood as an act of the Holy Spirit and created a Christian ritual that acknowledges the human soul's cry for a rite of passage.[7]

We can also learn from sources belonging to particular cultures or societies. Judaism has the bar mitzvah and bat mitzvah, the Southern states have the debutante ball, Latin America has the quinceañera, Africa has rites of passage, Native Americans have the vision quest—these are just a few of the coming-of-age ceremonies that our world offers. There are many more, and societies around the world also offer rituals for other life events. We can learn from them and utilize them in our Christian ritual creation.

How I Use Resources

Shedding light on one example of how I use these sources might be helpful. Friends recently requested a ritual to mark healing and renewal in their marriage and family. First, I spent time listening to them, learning about their marriage journey and their themes and desires for the ritual. Then I went to work. As it was related to marriage, I first looked at the BCP and Orthodox marriage ceremonies to see if there was anything I could use there. I jotted down themes and cut and pasted prayers, with citations, into a document. Then I did a general internet search for marriage blessings and found the betrothal liturgy of the Byzantine-Ruthenian Catholic Church; their prayer over the rings appealed to me because the couple had already purchased new rings for the ritual.[8] I also investigated biblical readings for funerals, as one of the themes of the ritual was to be death and resurrection; they were marking the end of portions of the past and the journey into newness.

I spent a great deal of time thinking through an appropriate symbol in addition to the rings that would represent what they intended to mark. I suggested the symbol of river rocks for a number of reasons. Rocks are a symbol of stability and are smoothed and formed by currents; this ritual would celebrate the stability of their marriage even as it has been formed by rough currents. Piles of rocks called cairns mark hiking trails where there are no trees; and in the Bible, they are used as altars (see, e.g., Josh. 4:1–8). This ritual would mark and help them remember a high point on their journey of marriage. They would write or engrave something meaningful on a good-sized rock found in a local riverbed. I also chatted with them about whom to invite and suggested they do the ritual where they were married.

Finally, I sat down and wrote the ritual. I entitled it "Marking a Mountain with a View on the Journey of Marriage," as this was appropriate to their story. I explained the symbol and its use in the ritual. It was mostly a rearrangement and adaptation of common marriage words and prayers, many from the BCP, since they are Episcopalian. I wrote some special blessings and included specific instruction for the symbols. I finished it and, with some trepidation, sent it.

I am still getting used to sharing my rituals with the world. I am not generally a timid person but can become timid with rituals because it is a deep part of my creativity. I feel vulnerable to rejection and can feel as if they are rejecting *me*, not a ritual that I created. Right now my goal is to share more often so that I can get used to the feelings of vulnerability and possible rejection. That is why I write this book.

Acknowledgments

It takes a village to write a book.

As I recognize my village, I touch my forehead, chest, and shoulders: Father, Son, Holy Spirit, in the shape of the cross. I mark myself as God's through the cross of Christ and offer thanks for the people, for my village. I join countless Christians in history who thank God in the same way.

Every morning, I try to write three things I'm grateful for. Each one always makes me smile and feel more at peace because I am full. Even when life feels awful, it is simultaneously true that I am full. I have a village for whom I am grateful.

When Katelyn Beaty with Brazos Press sought me out at a Missio Alliance conference in 2019, she made me feel valuable as a writer and she encouraged my voice. Her guidance in the writing process and final editing work have been invaluable, and I continue to be impressed with the entire Brazos Press team. Thank you.

Fadi and Badia watched my three-month-old son when I first presented on this book's topic at an academic conference in 2014. That presentation for the Biblical Worship section began the journey to today's finished product, though I had only been directing the *Woman* rite of passage for three years at the time.

The *Woman* leadership team and mentors—including Wanda, Wanda, Lisa, Christina, Debbie, Eugenia, Rebecca, Yolanda, Xelena, Mariela, Katherine, and Joanna—invested in *Woman* and therefore invested in this book. I am grateful to you and to all *Woman* participants for allowing us to journey together.

I was delighted to join the TheoPsych cohort in 2020. I still haven't met most of you in person, but I am grateful for the many conversations about rituals and psychology. Blueprint 1543 was generous enough to offer a grant to help fund this book. Many thanks to Justin, Rebecca, and Holly. Special thanks to Sarey and her team for a fun video project in Brooklyn.

TheoPsych put me in contact with amazing psychology professors who answered my emails loaded with questions about neuropsychology, embodiment, psychology of religion, and developmental psychology. Pamela, Brad, Kutter, and Bill, I couldn't believe you would take the time to answer me; you hardly knew me. Your investment has paid off. Thank you.

To those who gave me special insight into their journeys: Margie, Catherine, Kevin and Katie, Kyle and Angela. You helped me create.

I've saved the most important for last. To Deborah, my TA. You were willing to listen to me verbally process ideas so that they could form something cohesive. You taught me Endnote, you edited the manuscript, you dedicated time and effort to this work. Thank you. You are so much more than an assistant.

And now, to my family. There is no one else with whom I would rather journey through so many beginnings, middles, and ends. Ghiath, thank you for your unwavering support and for giving me time and space to work without interruption. Jaohar and Naraam, you are delightful. You make everything worthwhile.

May our rituals empower us all to become who we are created to be!

Notes

Introduction

1. As of September 2022, Nyack College is now Alliance University. It was Nyack at the time of the event described here.

2. The rite of passage was also formed by my dissertation research: Amy F. Davis, "Rites of Passage for Women in Evangelical Christianity: A Theological and Ritual Analysis" (PhD diss., Drew University, 2010).

3. Theresa A. Rando, "Creating Therapeutic Rituals in the Psychotherapy of the Bereaved," *Psychotherapy* 22 (1985): 236–40, quoted in Joanne Cacciatore and Melissa Flint, "Mediating Grief: Postmortem Ritualization after Child Death," *Journal of Loss and Trauma* 17, no. 2 (2012): 163.

4. The idea of God story and human story are from Mark Earey, *Worship That Cares: An Introduction to Pastoral Liturgy* (London: SCM, 2012), 45–48.

5. On both sexual intercourse and elimination on the toilet, see Lauren F. Winner, *Mudhouse Sabbath: An Invitation to a Life of Spiritual Discipline* (Brewster, MA: Paraclete, 2016), 68–69.

6. Rona Shapiro, "A Blessing for a First Sexual Experience," Ritual Well, accessed February 6, 2021, https://www.ritualwell.org/ritual/blessing-first -sexual-experience. It is significant to note that the Roman Catholic Church made headlines in 2009 because their *Prayer Book for Spouses* (London: Incorporated Catholic Truth Society, 2009) contained a prayer for couples before sexual intercourse; reviews were mixed.

7. Tom Faw Driver, *Liberating Rites: Understanding the Transformative Power of Ritual* (Boulder, CO: Westview, 1998), xi.

8. Ronald L. Grimes, *Deeply into the Bone: Re-inventing Rites of Passage* (Berkeley: University of California Press, 2002), 7.

9. "Free-church Protestant" is a term referring to multiple Protestant traditions that have common characteristics. Christopher J. Ellis defines free-church worship in *Gathering: A Theology and Spirituality of Worship in Free Church Tradition* (London: SCM, 2004). Theologically, free churches tend to

be evangelical and linked both to ecumenism and other Christian groups who are not ecumenical (7). Their worship is "free," without a prayer book (6), different in each local church, and "open to the extempore guidance of the Holy Spirit" (27). As such, this designation may include Baptists, Congregationalists, Methodists, Pentecostals, nondenominational churches, and more (25).

10. This phrase is from the (Episcopalian) Book of Common Prayer's Ash Wednesday service, which contains the words "to make a right beginning of repentance." "Ash Wednesday," in *The Book of Common Prayer and Administration of the Sacraments and Other Rites and Ceremonies of the Church Together with the Psalter or Psalms of David* (n.p.: Seabury, 1979), 265, available at https://bcponline.org.

Chapter 1 Ritual Transforms and Embodies

1. Tom Faw Driver, *Liberating Rites: Understanding the Transformative Power of Ritual* (Boulder, CO: Westview, 1998), 93, 167.

2. Ronald L. Grimes, *The Craft of Ritual Studies* (New York: Oxford University Press, 2013), 319.

3. Leonard J. Vander Zee, *Christ, Baptism and the Lord's Supper: Recovering the Sacraments for Evangelical Worship* (Downers Grove, IL: InterVarsity, 2004), 45–52.

4. John Damascene, *St. John Damascene on Holy Images, Followed by Three Sermons on the Assumption*, trans. Mary H. Allies (London: Thomas Baker, 1898), 15–16.

5. Francis Brown, S. R. Driver, and Charles A. Briggs, *Brown Driver Briggs Hebrew and English Lexicon* (n.p.: Snowball, 2010), 997b.

6. Brad D. Strawn and Warren Brown, *Enhancing Christian Life: How Extended Cognition Augments Religious Community* (Downers Grove, IL: IVP Academic, 2020), 32.

7. Frederick W. Danker and Kathryn Krug, *The Concise Greek-English Lexicon of the New Testament* (Chicago: University of Chicago Press, 2009), 305.

8. I write more about this prayer in chap. 4.

9. Driver, *Liberating Rites*, 184–85.

10. Grimes, *Craft of Ritual Studies*, 313.

11. Driver, *Liberating Rites*, xi.

12. This union of time—past, present, and future—is called "anamnesis," particularly when we refer to the union that occurs during the Lord's Supper, or Eucharist. This idea will be explored more deeply in chap. 3.

13. Grimes, *Craft of Ritual Studies*, 315. Grimes also states, "Ritual is simultaneously cognitive, emotional, and physical" (323).

14. Driver, *Liberating Rites*, 174–75.

15. Susan Marie Smith, *Caring Liturgies: The Pastoral Power of Christian Ritual* (Minneapolis: Fortress, 2012), 6, citing Catherine Bell, *Ritual Theory, Ritual Practice* (Oxford: Oxford University Press, 1992), 82.

16. Smith, *Caring Liturgies*, 5–6.

17. John Medina, "Rule #10: Vision Trumps All Other Senses," Brain Rules (website), accessed January 19, 2023, http://www.brainrules.net/vision.

18. Brené Brown, "Creativity, Surrender, and Aesthetic Force, with Dr. Sarah Lewis," *Dare to Lead with Brené Brown*, podcast, January 25, 2021, 1:11:28 (comments begin at 26:13), https://brenebrown.com/podcast/brene -with-dr-sarah-lewis-on-creativity-surrender-and-aesthetic-force.

19. Ronald L. Grimes, *Deeply into the Bone: Re-inventing Rites of Passage* (Berkeley: University of California Press, 2000), 6–7.

20. Strawn and Brown, *Enhancing Christian Life*, 47.

21. Grimes, *Craft of Ritual Studies*, 242.

22. Grimes, *Craft of Ritual Studies*, 243.

23. Arnold van Gennep, *The Rites of Passage*, trans. Monika B. Vizedom and Gabrielle L. Caffee (Chicago: University of Chicago Press, 1960).

24. This was primarily because menarche occurs at different times for different individuals. The male rite had a set time for groups of boys.

25. Bruce Lincoln, *Emerging from the Chrysalis: Rituals of Women's Initiation* (New York: Oxford University Press, 1991), 105, 107–8.

26. Criticism exists about the "neatness" of the three-part rite-of-passage scheme. Though portions of Western culture may reject belief in the Trinity, it nonetheless seems that we tend to see things in threes. For our purposes we will acknowledge that the scheme does not necessarily fully describe rites of passage yet is still useful as a tool for description.

27. *Communitas* is the special nonhierarchical community created when individuals share a liminal state. See also Victor W. Turner, *The Ritual Process: Structure and Anti-structure* (New York: Aldine de Gruyter, 1995), 96–97. Interestingly, Turner states that "numerical limitations [exist] that seem to be set upon groups that maximize existential communitas" (142). That is, *communitas* exists best in smaller groups, though he is not specific as to the best number. We explore specific numbers in chap. 5 using Priya Parker's work *The Art of Gathering*.

28. Grimes, *Deeply into the Bone*, 121.

29. For centuries, marriage was a rite of passage that marked adulthood. Recent demographics show, however, that in much of Western society, marriage no longer plays that role. Some never marry, and for those who do, marriage begins later in life than it once did, and divorce is common. "Unmarried and Single Americans Week: September 18–24, 2022," United States Census Bureau, September 18, 2022, https://www.census.gov/newsroom/sto ries/unmarried-single-americans-week.html.

30. Amy F. Davis, "Rites of Passage for Women in Evangelical Christianity: A Theological and Ritual Analysis" (PhD diss., Drew University, 2010).

31. Amy F. Davis Abdallah, *The Book of Womanhood* (Eugene, OR: Cascade Books, 2015), 13. More information on this rite of passage and its values can be found in this book as well as the author's personal website

(http://amyfdavisabdallah.com) and the site for the rite of passage (https://nyackwoman.wordpress.com).

32. Barbara Veith and Alice Cooney Frelinghuysen, "Women China Decorators," Metropolitan Museum of Art (website), April 2013, https://www.metmuseum.org/toah/hd/woch/hd_woch.htm.

33. "Absence of Rites of Passage," *Encyclopedia of World Problems and Human Potential*, http://encyclopedia.uia.org/en/problem/absence-rites-passage, quoted in Grimes, *Deeply into the Bone*, 91.

34. Hippolytus, *The Apostolic Tradition of Hippolytus*, trans. Burton Scott Easton (Cambridge: Cambridge University Press, 1934), 91, available at https://www.gutenberg.org/files/61614/61614-h/61614-h.htm.

Chapter 2 You Already Ritualize (You Just Don't Call It That)

1. John Meyendorff, *Marriage: An Orthodox Perspective* (Crestwood, NY: St. Vladimir's Seminary Press, 2000), 23.

2. Everett Ferguson, *Backgrounds of Early Christianity* (Grand Rapids: Eerdmans, 2009), 74.

3. Ferguson, *Backgrounds of Early Christianity*, 75.

4. "God fearers" were those who worshiped with the Jews but were not full proselytes, probably because they had not been circumcised. Cornelius the centurion (Acts 10) is described as one, and the Ethiopian eunuch is presumed to be one. As a eunuch, he could not be circumcised.

5. This idea that a ritual is a play that enacts meaning will be explored in chap. 3 as the aesthetic distance of ritual.

6. While many have strong feelings for or against infant baptism, it is important to note that these practices were developed because of biblical interpretation, theological tenets, and practical considerations. Our concern here is not to advocate for one or the other; it is simply to show that church rituals are invented.

7. Frank C. Senn, *Christian Liturgy: Catholic and Evangelical* (Minneapolis: Fortress, 1998), 222.

8. Laura De Jong, "Body and Soul: Baptismal Solidarity at a Funeral," *Calvin Theological Journal* 56, no. 1 (2021): 67–68.

9. Dru Johnson, *Human Rites: The Power of Rituals, Habits, and Sacraments* (Grand Rapids: Eerdmans, 2019), 4.

10. Johnson, *Human Rites*, 5.

11. These actions are from the following example ritual: "Alpha Kappa Alpha Initiation Ritual," Argus Foundation, accessed April 10, 2023, https://www.stichtingargus.nl/vrijmetselarij/g/alphakappaalpha_r.html.

12. Michael Karlin, "Coming of Age on the Street: Ritual Invention and the Sacred in American Gang Initiation Rituals," *Council of Societies for the Study of Religion Bulletin* 37, no. 3 (2008): 60.

13. Karlin, "Coming of Age," 62.

14. George P. Fletcher, "Update the Pledge," *New York Times*, December 6, 1992, 19, quoted by Catherine M. Bell, *Ritual: Perspectives and Dimensions* (New York: Oxford University Press, 1997), 230.

15. Jayne A. Fulkerson et al., "Longitudinal Associations between Family Dinner and Adolescent Perceptions of Parent–Child Communication among Racially Diverse Urban Youth," *Journal of Family Psychology* 24, no. 3 (2010): 261.

16. Evan Imber-Black, "Ritual Themes in Family and Family Therapy," in *Rituals in Families and Family Therapy*, ed. Evan Imber-Black, Janine Roberts, and Richard A. Whiting (New York: Norton, 2003), 53.

17. Imber-Black, "Ritual Themes," 53–87.

18. Tish Harrison Warren, *Liturgy of the Ordinary: Sacred Practices in Everyday Life* (Downers Grove, IL: InterVarsity, 2016), 141.

19. Warren, *Liturgy of the Ordinary*, 141.

20. See the "Liminal Times" ritual in chap. 7.

21. Tickle has three volumes in the set, for different seasons of the year. The work is currently published by Image.

22. "The Divine Hours," Vineyard Church Ann Arbor (website), accessed August 22, 2022, https://annarborvineyard.org/resources/pray-the-divine -hours.

23. Peter Bol, interview by Laurie Santos, "Happiness Lessons of the Ancients: Confucius," *The Happiness Lab with Dr. Laurie Santos*, podcast, April 26, 2021, 38:34 (comments begin at 13:51), https://www.pushkin.fm /podcasts/the-happiness-lab-with-dr-laurie-santos/happiness-lessons-of-the -ancients-confucius.

24. Tish Harrison Warren, *Prayer in the Night: For Those Who Watch, Wait, or Weep* (Downers Grove, IL: InterVarsity, 2021); Rich Villodas, *The Deeply Formed Life: Five Transformative Values to Root Us in the Way of Jesus* (Colorado Springs: Waterbrook, 2020).

25. Laurie Santos, "The Power of a Made-Up Ritual," *The Happiness Lab with Dr. Laurie Santos*, podcast, May 11, 2020, 36:03 (comments at 26:02), https://www.pushkin.fm/podcasts/the-happiness-lab-with-dr-laurie-santos /the-power-of-a-made-up-ritual.

26. Phyllis Tickle, *The Divine Hours: Prayers for Autumn and Wintertime* (New York: Doubleday, 2000); Tickle, *The Divine Hours: Prayers for Springtime: A Manual for Prayer* (New York: Doubleday, 2001); Tickle, *The Divine Hours: Prayers for Summertime: A Manual for Prayer* (New York: Doubleday, 2006).

27. This ritual does not lend itself to a key progression.

28. Tickle, *Divine Hours*, 135–36. Tish Harrison Warren has deeply examined the petition in her work *Prayer in the Night: For Those Who Work or Watch or Weep* (Downers Grove, IL: InterVarsity, 2021).

29. "A Home Blessing Liturgy," Restoration Anglican, 2021, https://resto rationmpls.org/blog/liturgy-for-home-blessing.

Chapter 3 How Rituals Help and Unite Us

1. Mary Elizabeth Kenel, "Ritual: Mediating Change," *Human Development* 32, no. 3 (Fall 2011): 22.

2. In chap. 8, I will address Pauline Boss's concept of ambiguous loss and discuss how ritual can help us process it. We have rituals for loss through death but need rituals for other types of loss.

3. Joanna Wojtkowiak, "Towards a Psychology of Ritual: A Theoretical Framework of Ritual Transformation in a Globalising World," *Culture and Psychology* 24, no. 4 (2018), https://doi.org/10.1177/1354067X18763797. See also Janine Roberts, "Setting the Frame: Definition, Functions, and Typology of Rituals," in *Rituals in Families and Family Therapy*, ed. Evan Imber-Black, Janine Roberts, and Richard A. Whiting (New York: Norton, 1988), 24.

4. D. A. Marshall, "Behavior, Belonging, and Belief: A Theory of Ritual Practice," *Sociological Theory* 20, no. 3 (2002), https://doi.org/10.1111/1467 -9558.00168.

5. Roberts, "Setting the Frame," 18 (emphasis original).

6. Wojtkowiak, "Towards a Psychology of Ritual," 467.

7. Wojtkowiak, "Towards a Psychology of Ritual" 467.

8. Kenel, "Ritual," 20.

9. Kenel, "Ritual," 21.

10. William Bridges and Susan Bridges, *Transitions: Making Sense of Life's Changes*, 40th anniv. ed. (New York: Hachette, 2019).

11. Sarah Demmrich and Uwe Wolfradt, "Personal Rituals in Adolescence: Their Role in Emotion Regulation and Identity Formation," *Journal of Empirical Theology* 31, no. 2 (2018): 234. See also the power of ritual to regulate emotions: Nicholas M. Hobson et al., "The Psychology of Rituals: An Intergrative Review and Process-Based Framework," *Personality and Social Psychology Review* 22, no. 3 (2018): 4–5.

12. Mary Douglas, *Purity and Danger: An Analysis of Concept of Pollution and Taboo* (New York: Routledge, 2005), 87–89.

13. Elizabeth A. Gassin and Timothy A. Sawchak, "Meaning, Performance, and Function of a Christian Forgiveness Ritual," *Journal of Ritual Studies* 22, no. 1 (2008): 44.

14. Hobson et al., "Psychology of Rituals," 6.

15. I elaborate more on Sabbath keeping in Amy F. Davis Abdallah, *The Book of Womanhood* (Eugene, OR: Cascade Books, 2015), chap. 14.

16. Michael I. Norton and Francesca Gino, "Rituals Alleviate Grieving for Loved Ones, Lovers, and Lotteries," *Journal of Experimental Psychology: General* 143, no. 1 (2014): 269.

17. Norton and Gino, "Rituals Alleviate Grieving," 271.

18. Patricia K. Suggs and Douglas J. Suggs, "The Understanding and Creation of Rituals: Enhancing the Life of Older Adults," *Journal of Religious Gerontology* 15, no. 3 (2003): 18.

19. Hobson et al., "Psychology of Rituals," 6–7.

20. Kenel, "Ritual," 22.

21. Wojtkowiak, "Towards a Psychology of Ritual," 470.

22. Susan Marie Smith, *Caring Liturgies: The Pastoral Power of Christian Ritual* (Minneapolis: Fortress, 2012), 4.

23. Smith, *Caring Liturgies*, 7.

24. Smith, *Caring Liturgies*, 7.

25. Smith, *Caring Liturgies*, 3.

26. Douglas, *Purity and Danger*, 116.

27. Tom Faw Driver, *Liberating Rites: Understanding the Transformative Power of Ritual* (Boulder, CO: Westview, 1998), 80.

28. Smith, *Caring Liturgies*, 6.

29. Smith, *Caring Liturgies*, 5.

30. Hobson et al., "Psychology of Rituals," 9.

31. Wojtkowiak, "Towards a Psychology of Ritual," 468.

32. Gassin and Sawchak, "Meaning, Performance, and Function," 44.

33. Hobson et al., "Psychology of Rituals," 18.

34. Roberts, "Setting the Frame," 17.

35. Roberts, "Setting the Frame," 19.

36. Catherine M. Bell, *Ritual Theory, Ritual Practice* (New York: Oxford University Press, 2009), 21–22.

37. Douglas, *Purity and Danger*, 78.

38. Evan Imber-Black and Janine Roberts, *Rituals for Our Times: Celebrating, Healing, and Changing Our Lives and Our Relationships* (New York: HarperCollins, 1992), 6.

39. Imber-Black and Roberts, *Rituals for Our Times*, 6.

40. Paul Tillich, *Theology of Culture*, ed. Robert C. Kimball (New York: Oxford University Press, 1959), 56.

41. Tillich, *Theology of Culture*, 56.

42. Wojtkowiak, "Towards a Psychology of Ritual," 467.

43. Wojtkowiak, "Towards a Psychology of Ritual," 467.

44. Michael Karlin, "Coming of Age on the Street: Ritual Invention and the Sacred in American Gang Initiation Rituals," *Council of Societies for the Study of Religion Bulletin* 37, no. 3 (2008): 61.

45. Karlin, "Coming of Age," 62.

46. Driver, *Liberating Rites*, 152.

47. Roy A. Rappaport, *Ecology, Meaning, and Religion* (Richmond, CA: North Atlantic Books, 1979), quoted in Tom Driver, *Liberating Rites*, 152.

48. Hobson et al., "Psychology of Rituals," 11.

49. That is, as long as they were honorably discharged and not convicted or in proceedings for a state or capital crime. For details, see "Military Funeral Honors Eligibilty," US Department of Defense, 2021, https://www.militaryonesource.mil/military-life-cycle/veterans-military-funeral-honors/eligibility.

50. Catherine Bell, *Ritual Theory, Ritual Practice*, 20, citing Emile Durkheim, *The Elementary Forms of Religious Life*, trans. J. W. Swain (New York: Free Press, 1965), 463ff.

51. A version of this ritual was previously published in Amy F. Davis Abdallah, "Embracing Ritual on Your Journey of Grief," Redbud Writers Guild, June 1, 2021, https://redbudwritersguild.com/embracing-ritual-on-your-journey-through-grief.

Chapter 4 Avoiding Powerless Rituals

1. Eric J. Tully, *Reading the Prophets as Christian Scripture: A Literary, Canonical, and Theological Introduction* (Grand Rapids: Baker Academic, 2022), 280. For more on this portion of Amos, see Thomas John Finley, *Joel, Amos, Obadiah*, Wycliffe Exegetical Commentary (Chicago: Moody, 1990), 220; R. Alan Fuhr, "True Worship versus False Worship: Worship in the Preexilic Minor Prophets," in *Biblical Worship: Theology for God's Glory*, ed. Benjamin K. Forrest, Walter C. Kaister Jr., and Vernon M. Whaley (Grand Rapids: Kregel Academic, 2021), 276–77.

2. Amy Peeler, "The Supper of the Lord: Goodness and Grace in 1 Corinthians 11:17–34," in *Sacraments and Christian Unity: Come, Let Us Eat Together*, ed. George Kalantzis and Marc Cortez (Downers Grove, IL: InterVarsity, 2018), 15.

3. I have been very brief here. For more information on the Corinthian Lord's Supper problem and its correction, see Peeler, "The Supper of the Lord"; Alan F. Johnson, *1 Corinthians* (Downers Grove, IL: InterVarsity, 2004), 201–14; Paul Gardner, *1 Corinthians* (Grand Rapids: Zondervan, 2018), 504–20.

4. Ronald L. Grimes, *Ritual Criticism: Case Studies in Its Practice, Essays on Its Theory*, Studies in Comparative Religion (Columbia: University of South Carolina Press, 1990), under "The Nature of Criticism."

5. Susan Marie Smith, *Christian Ritualizing and the Baptismal Process: Liturgical Explorations toward a Realized Baptismal Ecclesiology*, Princeton Theological Monograph Series (Eugene, OR: Pickwick, 2012), 7.

6. Smith, *Christian Ritualizing*, 14–54.

7. My guidance here does not restrict worship leading to the able-bodied. I am saying that when we all perform to the best of our individual abilities, participants' experience is enhanced.

8. Grimes, *Ritual Criticism*, under "Definitions of Ritual."

9. Susan Marie Smith goes into detail about attributes necessary for ritual planning in *Caring Liturgies: The Pastoral Power of Christian Ritual* (Minneapolis: Fortress, 2012), 46–51. My assumptions somewhat parallel her attributes of theological awareness, ethical acuity, and ecclesial connection.

10. Douglas McKelvey, *Every Moment Holy*, vol. 1 (Nashville: Rabbit Room, 2019); McKelvey, *Every Moment Holy*, vol. 2, *Death, Grief, and Hope* (Nashville: Rabbit Room, 2021).

11. This is the version of the prayer I learned in church, which seems unavailable online. Multiple slightly different versions exist, such as the one found here: "Lenten Prayer of St. Ephrem," Orthodox Church in America (website), accessed August 21, 2022, https://www.oca.org/orthodoxy/prayers/lenten-prayer-of-st.-ephrem.

12. "Ash Wednesday," in *The Book of Common Prayer and Administration of the Sacraments and Other Rites and Ceremonies of the Church Together with the Psalter or Psalms of David* (n.p.: Seabury, 1979), 265, available at https://bcponline.org.

13. Gordon Dalbey, *Healing the Masculine Soul: How God Restores Men to Real Manhood*, rev. ed. (Nashville: W Publishing, 2003), 30–32.

14. Dalbey, *Healing the Masculine Soul*, 37–41.

15. Amy F. Davis, "Rites of Passage for Women in Evangelical Christianity: A Theological and Ritual Analysis" (PhD diss., Drew University, 2010), 15, quoting Ronald L. Grimes, *Deeply into the Bone: Re-inventing Rites of Passage* (Berkeley: University of California Press, 2000), 11, 128.

16. Because I work with rites of passage, I have further recommendations that would help make the rite more effective. As the focus of this book is broader than rites of passage, they are not included here.

17. Grimes, *Deeply into the Bone*, 116.

Chapter 5 Pursuing Powerful Rituals

1. Victor Turner, *The Forest of Symbols: Aspect of Ndembu Ritual* (Ithaca, NY: Cornell University Press, 1967), cited in Janine Roberts, "Setting the Frame: Definition, Functions, and Typology of Rituals," in *Rituals in Families and Family Therapy*, ed. Evan Imber-Black, Janine Roberts, and Richard A. Whiting (New York: Norton, 1988), 7.

2. Perhaps you come from an ordinance-based tradition that is very skeptical of the power or blessing of "things." It must be stated, however, that most of the history of Christianity has been sacramental, which means believing God works through "things." There is a continuum, with different traditions believing in different degrees of power in the symbols.

3. Susan Marie Smith, *Caring Liturgies: The Pastoral Power of Christian Ritual* (Minneapolis: Fortress, 2012), 71, 74.

4. Priya Parker, *The Art of Gathering: How We Meet and Why It Matters* (New York: Riverhead, 2018), 52.

5. Parker, *Art of Gathering*, 51.

6. Parker, *Art of Gathering*, 53.

7. Parker, *Art of Gathering*, 55.

8. Parker, *Art of Gathering*, 58.

9. Ronald L. Grimes, *Deeply into the Bone: Re-inventing Rites of Passage* (Berkeley: University of California Press, 2000), 5.

10. Grimes, *Deeply into the Bone*, 6–7.

11. Grimes, *Deeply into the Bone*, 6.

12. Grimes, *Deeply into the Bone*, 6.

13. Tom Faw Driver, *Liberating Rites: Understanding the Transformative Power of Ritual* (Boulder, CO: Westview, 1998), 93.

14. Ronald L. Grimes, *Ritual Criticism: Case Studies in Its Practice, Essays on Its Theory*, Studies in Comparative Religion (Columbia: University of South Carolina Press, 1990), under "Scholarly Contexts and Practices."

15. Parker, *Art of Gathering*, 17.

16. See Amy F. Davis Abdallah, *The Book of Womanhood* (Eugene, OR: Cascade Books, 2015), chap. 8.

17. Parker, *Art of Gathering*, 3–4.

18. Parker, *Art of Gathering*, 31.

19. Parker, *Art of Gathering*, chap. 3.

20. Parker, *Art of Gathering*, 83–94.

21. The Higher Education Opportunity Program (HEOP) is a scholarship program for students who would not otherwise have access to higher education due to economic or educational disadvantage. For more information, see "Higher Education Opportunity Program (HEOP)," New York State Education Department, accessed August 21, 2022, http://www.nysed.gov/postsecondary-services/higher-education-opportunity-program-heop.

22. *Communitas* is Turner's term for a special community created by the liminal stage of a rite of passage.

23. I do not think that Christian womanhood is realized *only* through this rite of passage; there are other paths. However, requiring much from individuals tends to increase efficacy, so we do.

24. Grimes, *Deeply into the Bone*, 7.

25. Parker, *Art of Gathering*, 149.

26. Parker, *Art of Gathering*, 152, 55, 58.

27. I have written an article on that first year: Amy F. Davis Abdallah, "Development and Efficacy of a Rite of Passage for Evangelical Women," *Religious Education* 107, no. 5 (2012).

28. This sentence is the serenity prayer, used frequently in Alcoholics Anonymous and attributed to Reinhold Neibuhr.

Chapter 6 Ends

1. They also give each event a point value.

2. Saul McLeod, "Stress and Life Events," Simply Psychology, 2010, https://www.simplypsychology.org/SRRS.html.

3. Nancy K. Schlossberg, *Retire Smart, Retire Happy: Finding Your True Path in Life* (Washington, DC: American Psychological Association, 2003), 17–21.

4. Schlossberg, *Retire Smart*, 15.

5. William Bridges and Susan Mitchell Bridges, *Managing Transitions: Making the Most of Change*, 4th ed. (Boston: Da Capo Lifelong Books, 2016), 3.

6. William Bridges and Susan Bridges, *Transitions: Making Sense of Life's Changes*, 40th anniv. ed. (New York: Hachette, 2019), 11, 18.

7. Bridges and Bridges, *Transitions*, 10.

8. In the case of miscarriage and stillbirth, it is not enfranchised. I offer more on that later in the chapter.

9. Kenneth J. Doka, "Disenfranchised Grief in Historical and Cultural Perspective," in *Handbook of Bereavement Research and Practice: Advances in Theory and Intervention*, ed. Margaret S. Stroebe et al. (Washington, DC: American Psychological Association, 2008), 226.

10. Doka, "Disenfranchised Grief," 224, 228.

11. Doka, "Disenfranchised Grief," 224.

12. Doka's typologies of disenfranchised grief that relate to death are not our focus here, but they are worth exploring. See Doka, "Disenfranchised Grief," 229–34.

13. Doka, "Disenfranchised Grief," 234.

14. Judith L. M. McCoyd, Jeanne M. Koller, and Carolyn Ambler Walter, *Grief and Loss across the Lifespan: A Biopsychosocial Perspective*, 2nd ed. (New York: Springer, 2016), 1.

15. McCoyd, Koller, and Walter, *Grief and Loss*, 3.

16. Bridges and Bridges, *Transitions*, 112.

17. Bridges and Bridges, *Transitions*, 112–24.

18. Mark Searle, "The Journey of Conversion," *Worship* 54, no. 1 (1980): 39.

19. Searle, "Journey of Conversion," 39.

20. McCoyd, Koller, and Walter, *Grief and Loss*, 2, 6.

21. McCoyd, Koller, and Walter, *Grief and Loss*, 11.

22. McCoyd, Koller, and Walter, *Grief and Loss*, 17.

23. Bridges and Bridges, *Transitions*, 110–11.

24. Pauline Boss, *The Myth of Closure: Ambiguous Loss in a Time of Pandemic* (New York: Norton, 2022), under "Six Guidelines for the Resilience to Live with Loss."

25. Sofia Triliva, Anneke M. Sools, and Theofanis Philippas, "Using Narrative Futuring as a Means of Facing Liminal Employment Status and Space," *Qualitative Psychology* 9, no. 3 (2020): 1.

26. Susan A. David, *Emotional Agility: Get Unstuck, Embrace Change, and Thrive in Work and Life* (New York: Avery, 2016), under "The Upside of Anger (and Other Challenging Emotions)."

27. Boss, *Myth of Closure*, under "Revise Attachment."

28. Boss, *Myth of Closure*, under "Six Guidelines for the Resilience to Live with Loss."

29. Boss, *Myth of Closure*, under "Revise Attachment."

30. Amy F. Davis Abdallah, "Let's Create Divorce Ceremonies, Church!," Redbud Writers Guild, February 29, 2020, https://redbudwritersguild.com /lets-create-divorce-ceremonies-church.

31. Helen Russell, *How to Be Sad: Everything I've Learned about Getting Happier by Being Sad* (New York: HarperOne, 2021), xi.

32. Russell, *How to Be Sad*, xii.

33. McCoyd, Koller, and Walter, *Grief and Loss*, 40.

34. Doka, "Disenfranchised Grief," 226.

35. Joanne Cacciatore and Melissa Flint, "Mediating Grief: Postmortem Ritualization after Child Death," *Journal of Loss and Trauma* 17, no. 2 (2012): 159.

36. McCoyd, Koller, and Walter, *Grief and Loss*, 41. I am not sure why the authors assume only the mother feels the loss. In my experience both parents feel the loss, and sometimes the father feels it even more than the mother.

37. Puneet Singh, Kearsley Stewart, and Scott Moses, "Pastoral Care Following Pregnancy Loss: The Role of Ritual," *Journal of Pastoral Care and Counseling* 58, no. 1–2 (Spring 2004): 47.

38. Doka, "Disenfranchised Grief," 227.

39. John 1:25–26; Job 19:25–26. "The Burial of the Dead: Rite One," in *The Book of Common Prayer and Administration of the Sacraments and Other Rites and Ceremonies of the Church Together with the Psalter or Psalms of David* (n.p.: Seabury, 1979), 265, available at https://bcponline.org.

40. This is a conflation of multiple prayers: "For a Departed Child after a Miscarriage," in *The Ancient Faith Prayer Book*, ed. Vassilios Papavassiliou (Chesterton, IN: Ancient Faith, 2014), 135; and "At the Burial of a Child," and "The Burial of the Dead: Rite One," in *Book of Common Prayer*, 470, available at https://bcponline.org.

41. Some portions of this prayer are adapted from a prayer called "For a Woman after Miscarriage," in *Ancient Faith Prayer Book*, 134.

42. "Question 1," New City Catechism, accessed September 4, 2022, http://newcitycatechism.com/new-city-catechism/#1.

43. "The Burial of the Dead: Rite Two," in *Book of Common Prayer*, 498, available at https://bcponline.org.

44. This is adapted from "The Reconciliation of a Penitent," in *Book of Common Prayer*, 447–52, available at https://bcponline.org.

45. This can be adapted for marriages without children.

46. "Ministration to the Sick," in *Book of Common Prayer*, 456, available at https://bcponline.org.

Chapter 7 Middles

1. Arnold van Gennep, *The Rites of Passage*, trans. Monika B. Vizedom and Gabrielle L. Caffee (Chicago: University of Chicago Press, 1960), 15–25.

2. Cited in Ronald L. Grimes, *Deeply into the Bone: Re-inventing Rites of Passage* (Berkeley: University of California Press, 2000), 121–22.

3. Victor W. Turner, *The Ritual Process: Structure and Anti-structure* (New York: Aldine de Gruyter, 1995), 145.

4. Turner, *Ritual Process*, 146, 150.

5. Luke 8:1–3 names women (likely disciples) who funded Jesus's ministry; in Luke 10, Jesus sends out the seventy-two, who take nothing with them and are dependent on townspeople for everything; Jesus's statement that "foxes have dens and birds have nests, but the Son of Man has no place to lay his head" (Luke 9:58) points to the liminal state of wandering in which Jesus lived and leads many to conclude he had no home.

6. Sampson S. Ndoga, "Reading Psalm 13 as a Strategy for the Cathartic Release of Negative Emotion," *Old Testament Essays* 34, no. 1 (2021): 258.

7. I write about the meaning of Christian womanhood in Amy F. Davis Abdallah, *The Book of Womanhood* (Eugene, OR: Cascade Books, 2015).

8. Brown frequently mentions vulnerability in her work. Her thoughts were first broadcast to the world in Brené Brown, "The Power of Vulnerability," TED Talk, TEDxHouston, January 3, 2011, 20:49, https://www.ted.com/talks/brene_brown_the_power_of_vulnerability. The video has over sixty million views.

9. Dru Johnson, *Human Rites: The Power of Rituals, Habits, and Sacraments* (Grand Rapids: Eerdmans, 2019), 32.

10. Pauline Boss, *The Myth of Closure: Ambiguous Loss in a Time of Pandemic* (New York: Norton, 2022), under "Clearer Losses That May Still Have Some Ambiguity and Uncertainty."

11. Two types of ambiguous loss exist: physical and psychological. Physical ones are those with no proof of death, and an example of a psychological one is a person loving someone who, due to dementia, can no longer recognize him or her. Boss, *Myth of Closure*, under "Types of Ambiguous Loss."

12. Boss, *Myth of Closure*, under "Ambiguous Losses Due to COVID-19."

13. William Bridges and Susan Bridges, *Transitions: Making Sense of Life's Changes*, 40th anniv. ed. (New York: Hachette, 2019), 137–38.

14. Bridges and Bridges, *Transitions*, 158.

15. Michael F. Bird, *Introducing Paul: The Man, His Mission, and His Message* (Downers Grove, IL: InterVarsity, 2008), 31.

16. "Unmarried and Single Americans Week: September 18–24, 2022," United States Census Bureau, September 18, 2022, https://www.census.gov/newsroom/stories/unmarried-single-americans-week.html.

17. Claire Crisp, *Waking Mathilda: A Memoir of Childhood Narcolepsy* (n.p.: Palace Gate, 2017), 73–82.

18. Claire Crisp, interview with Mark Labberton, "Claire Crisp on Narcolepsy," *Conversing*, podcast, episode 86, November 17, 2020, 38:48, https://fullerstudio.fuller.edu/podcast/claire-crisp-on-narcolepsy.

19. Psalm 88 is the only lament psalm that does not resolve.

20. June F. Dickie, "What 'Persuades' God to Respond to the Psalmist's Cry? Use of Rhetorical Devices Related to 'Vows of Future Praise' in Some Psalms of Lament," *Old Testament Essays* 34, no. 3 (2021): 748–50.

21. Dickie, "What 'Persuades' God," 749.

22. Dickie, "What 'Persuades' God," 749.

23. Tish Harrison Warren, *Prayer in the Night: For Those Who Work or Watch or Weep* (Downers Grove, IL: InterVarsity, 2021), 94.

24. Warren, *Prayer in the Night*, 95.

25. Warren, *Prayer in the Night*, 95–96.

26. Arthur W. Frank, "Just Listening: Narrative and Deep Illness," *Families, Systems, and Health* 16, no. 3 (Fall 1998): 197–212.

27. Boss, *Myth of Closure*, under "Six Guidelines for the Resilience to Live with Loss."

28. Boss, *Myth of Closure*, under "Finding Meaning."

29. Kate Bowler, *Everything Happens for a Reason and Other Lies I've Loved* (New York: Random House, 2018).

30. Boss, *Myth of Closure*, under "The Myth of Closure."

31. Joan Huyser-Honig and Barbara J. Newman, "Universal Design, Vertical Habits, and Inclusive Worship," Calvin Institute of Christian Worship, July 1, 2015, https://worship.calvin.edu/resources/resource-library/universal -design-vertical-habits-and-inclusive-worship.

32. Boss, *Myth of Closure*, under "Six Guidelines for the Resilience to Live with Loss."

33. Boss, *Myth of Closure*, under "Normalize Ambivalence."

34. Boss, *Myth of Closure*, under "Adjust Mastery."

35. Boss, *Myth of Closure*, under "Reconstruct Identity."

36. While I cite Tierce, I first encountered this article in Tish Harrison Warren's *Prayer in the Night*, under "Keep Watch, Dear Lord: Pain and Presence." Some of my thought here is formed by Warren.

37. Merritt Tierce, "At Sea," *Paris Review*, November 18, 2016, https:// www.theparisreview.org/blog/2016/11/18/at-sea.

38. Tierce, "At Sea."

39. Julian of Norwich, *Revelations of Divine Love* 27, trans. Grace Warrack (Grand Rapids: Christian Classics Ethereal Library), 55, https://ccel.org /ccel/julian/revelations/revelations.xiv.i.html.

40. Amy Cuddy has done extensive work on power poses, as shown in her TED Talk: "Your Body Language May Shape Who You Are," TED Talk, TED Global 2012, 20:46, https://www.ted.com/talks/amy_cuddy_your_body _language_may_shape_who_you_are. She responds to skeptics in "Inside the Debate about Power Posing: Q&A with Amy Cuddy," interview by David Biello, Ideas.TED.com, February 22, 2017, https://ideas.ted.com/inside-the -debate-about-power-posing-a-q-a-with-amy-cuddy.

Chapter 8 Beginnings

1. I cannot write that all Christian traditions do this, because I know of at least one tradition that does not practice baptism: the Salvation Army churches.

2. Helen Russell, *How to Be Sad: Everything I've Learned about Getting Happier by Being Sad* (New York: HarperOne, 2021), 111, 120.

3. Isca Salzberger-Wittenberg, *Experiencing Endings and Beginnings* (London: Karnac Books, 2013), 2.

4. William Bridges and Susan Bridges, *Transitions: Making Sense of Life's Changes*, 40th anniv. ed. (New York: Hachette, 2019), 169.

5. John Galsworthy, *Over the River* (London: William Heinemann, 1933), 4, cited in Bridges and Bridges, *Transitions*, 163.

6. Bridges and Bridges, *Transitions*, 169–70.

7. Salzberger-Wittenberg, *Experiencing Endings and Beginnings*, 1.

8. Salzberger-Wittenberg, *Experiencing Endings and Beginnings*, 16.

9. Impostor phenomenon is also called "impostor syndrome." An article I wrote explains my preference for "phenomenon," discusses differences along lines of sex and race, and examines the presence of the phenomenon in Christianity. Amy F. Davis Abdallah, "Female Christian Responses to Contexts of Imposed Impostorism," *TheoLogica: An International Journal for Philosophy of Religion and Philosophical Theology* 6, no. 1 (2022).

10. Bridges and Bridges, *Transitions*, 175.

11. The beginning of palliative care could also be considered a liminal ritual for the terminally ill. It is another illustration of the fact that ends, middles, and beginnings are not watertight, separate compartments but, rather, sometimes happen at the same time.

12. Peter A. Clark, "The Transition between Ending Medical Treatment and Beginning Palliative Care: The Need for a Ritual Response," *Worship* 72, no. 4 (1998): 345.

13. Clark, "Transition between Ending Medical Treatment," 345.

14. Clark, "Transition between Ending Medical Treatment," 348–49.

15. Salzberger-Wittenberg, *Experiencing Endings and Beginnings*, 2.

16. Bridges and Bridges, *Transitions*, 162–63.

17. Bridges and Bridges, *Transitions*, 161.

18. Judith L. M. McCoyd, Jeanne M. Koller, and Carolyn Ambler Walter, *Grief and Loss across the Lifespan: A Biopsychosocial Perspective*, 2nd ed. (New York: Springer, 2016), 240.

19. "Holy Baptism," in *The Book of Common Prayer and Administration of the Sacraments and Other Rites and Ceremonies of the Church Together with the Psalter or Psalms of David* (n.p.: Seabury, 1979), available at https://bcponline.org.

20. In the same way that I am not ready to begin the new year until after I have created my "Summer Adventure Book" with my kids, this ritual beginning is best built on a previously ritualized ending of what came before.

Appendix: Exploring Our Sources

1. Douglas McKelvey, *Every Moment Holy*, vol. 1 (Nashville: Rabbit Room, 2019); McKelvey, *Every Moment Holy*, vol. 2, *Death, Grief, and Hope* (Nashville: Rabbit Room, 2021).

2. An online version of the 1979 Book of Common Prayer is available at https://bcponline.org.

3. "Occasional Prayers," Antiochian Orthodox Christian Archdiocese of North America (website), http://ww1.antiochian.org/orthodox-prayers /occasional-prayers.

4. "Online Prayer Book," Transfiguration of Our Savior Greek Orthodox Church (website), https://www.transchurch.org/ourfaith/prayers.

5. "Prayers for Orthodox Christians," Orthodox Church in America (website), https://www.oca.org/orthodoxy/prayers.

6. I have also found helpful *The Ancient Faith Prayer Book*, ed. Vassilios Papavassiliou (Chesterton, IN: Ancient Faith, 2014).

7. Gordon Dalbey, *Healing the Masculine Soul: How God Restores Men to Real Manhood*, rev. ed. (Nashville: W Publishing, 2003), 30.

8. "The Ritual of Marriage with Divine Liturgy," Patronage of the Mother of God Catholic Church, 2012, https://static1.squarespace.com/static/5180 c403e4b05de3eed18564/t/52f6d3d2e4b0ec7646d008bb/1391907794303/The +Ritual+of+Marriage+_letter+size__complete_.pdf.